TSD RALLYING WITH A PROGRAMMABLE CALCULATOR

BY LARRY REID

MODERN AUTOMOTIVE SERIES

TAB BOOKS

BLUE RIDGE SUMMIT, PA. 17214

FIRST EDITION

FIRST PRINTING—MAY 1978

Copyright © 1978 by TAB BOOKS

Printed in the United States
of America

Reproduction or publication of the content in any manner, without express permission of the publisher, is prohibited. No liability is assumed with respect to the use of the information herein.

Library of Congress Cataloging in Publication Data

Reid, Larry.
  TSD rallying with a programmable calculator.

  (Modern sports car series)
  Includes index.
    1. Automobile rallies—Computer programs. 3. Calculating-
    machines. I. Title.
GV1029.2.R44   796.7'2'02854   7-19125
ISBN 0-8306-9977-5
ISBN 0-8306-2043-5 pbk.

Contents

Acknowledgements — 6

Preface — 7

About the Author — 14

Part I
The Hewlett-Packard HP-25
Programmable Pocket Calculator — 15

1 Getting Acquainted with the HP-25 — 15
Programmability—The Keyboard—The Switches—The Registers—The Automatic Memory Stack—The Memory Storage Registers—Storage-Register Arithmetic—The Program-Step Register—The Last-x Register—Reverse Polish Notation—The Display—The Power Supply—Calculating with the HP-25

2 Navigational Arithmetic — 42
The Time-Speed-Distance Equation—The Odometer Check—The Correction Factors—Special Problems—The Average of the Averages—Analyzing Equations and Formulas—Percentages—"Phantom Car" Problems

3 Programming the HP-25 — 32
Program-Building—Program Checking and Debugging: The Keycodes—Data Entries and Program Initialization—Entering Negative Values—Iterative Programs—Unconditional Branching—Conditional Branching—More About Data Entries

4 HP-25 Rally Navigation Programs   54
HP-25 Average-Speed Navigation Program I—HP-25 Average-Speed Navigation Program II—HP-25 Average-Speed Navigation Program III—The Odometer Check—No Odometer Error—Other Distance Units—Time-Based Route Instructions—Simultaneous Displays—HP-25 Navigation Program II Modified for Simultaneous Display of Distance and Time—HP-25 Navigation Program III Modified for Simultaneous Display of Distance and Time

5 Testing the HP-25 Rally Programs   73

6 Unmaking Mistakes   81
Recovering After Getting Lost—Changing Speed at the Wrong Place—When You've Pressed the Wrong Button

7 Rally Scoring Programs for the HP-25   87
HP-25 Scoring Program I—HP-25 Maximum-Penalty Scoring Program IA—HP-25 Scoring Program II—HP-25 Maximum-Penalty Scoring Program IIA—Checking Out the Scoring Programs—HP-25 Checkpoint-by-Checkpoint Scoring Program III

**Part II
The Texas Instruments SR-56
Programmable Pocket Calculator**   101

---

8 Getting Acquainted with the SR-56   101
Programmability—A Word About Algebraic Notation—The Keyboard—The Switches—The Display—The Registers—Calculating with the SR-56

9 Navigational Arithmetic   120
The Time-Speed-Distance Equation—The Odometer Check—The Correction Factors—Special Problems—The Average of the Averages—Percentages—"Phantom Car" Problems

10 Programming the SR-56 — 127
Constructing a Program—Perfecting a Program—Time-Conversion Routines—Subroutines

11 SR-56 Rally Navigation Programs — 139
SR-56 Average-Speed Navigation Program I—SR-56 Average-Speed Navigation Program IA—SR-56 Average-Speed Navigation Program II—SR-56 Average-Speed Navigation Program IIA—Time-Based Route Directions—SR-56 Supplementary Routine for Time-Based Instructions—Simultaneous Displays—SR-56 Average-Speed Navigation Program I Modified for Simultaneous Display of Distance and Time—SR-56 Average-Speed Navigation Program IA Modified for Simultaneous Display of Distance and Time

12 Testing the SR-56 Rally Programs — 163

13 Unmaking Mistakes — 175
Recovering After Getting Lost—Changing Speed at the Wrong Place—When You've Pressed the Wrong Button

14 Rally Scoring Programs for the SR-56 — 179
SR-56 Scoring Program I—SR-56 Scoring Program IA—SR-56 Scoring Program II—SR-56 Scoring Program IIA—Checking Out the Scoring Programs—SR-56 Scoring Program III

Appendix — 190
Time-Speed-Distance Formulas—Correction Factors—"Phantom Car" Formulas—HP-25 Rally Navigation Programs—HP-25 Rally Navigation Program I—HP-25 Rally Navigation Program II—HP-25 Rally Navigation Program III—HP-25 Rally Navigation Program I Modified for Time-Based Route Instructions—SR-56 Rally Navigation Programs—SR-56 Rally Navigation Program I—SR-56 Rally Navigation Program IA—SR-56 Supplementary Routine for Time-Based Instructions—SR-56 Rally Navigation Program II—SR-56 Rally Navigation Program IIA—HP-25 Scoring Programs—HP-25 Scoring Program I—HP-25 Maximum-Penalty Scoring Program IA—HP-25 Hours and Decimal Minutes Scoring Program II—HP-25 Maximum Penalty Scoring Program IIA—SR-56 Scoring Programs—SR-56 Scoring Program I—SR-56 Scoring Program IA—SR-56 Scoring Program II—SR-56 Scoring Program IIA—SR-56 Scoring Program III — Postscript

Index — 222

For Joan, who did not say, "Not again!"

Acknowledgements

The author is much indebted to John B. Sturrock, M.D., of Boston, for introducing him to the HP-25 pocket electronic calculator, for pointing out its adaptability to rallying and suggesting a program, and for his help and encouragement; and to the Hewlett-Packard organization, in particular Stanwood E. Lehman, Consumer Sales Engineer, for their cooperation and assistance in furnishing the HP-25 pictures and diagrams used here and in reviewing Part I of the manuscript for accuracy. Thanks are due also to Reed Trask, Manager, Worldwide Press Relations, Texas Instruments Incorporated, for providing the illustration of, and technical information about, the SR-56.

Other TAB Books by the author:

No. 2014 *Larry Reid's New Rally Tables*
No. 2017 *New Guide to Rallying*
No. 2040 *Accessories for Your Sports Car*

Preface

EVER SINCE sports car rallying made its way from Europe to the United States a few years after the end of World War II, rallyists have searched continuously for better ways of solving the ever-present average-speed problem. Hundreds of times during a rally, contestants have to ask, "How long should it have taken us to get here at the stated speed?" They want not only accurate answers but fast answers; less time spent on doing arithmetic means more time spendable on following the route.

Navigators have attacked the time-speed-distance equation by many methods and with many different aids to calculating. The earliest tools were pencil and paper, buttressed perhaps with a slide rule. It would be hard to guess how many square miles of timberland went to make the paper on which all those numbers were so frantically scribbled. In time the tedium inspired some manufactured assistances for the overworked navigator. Early on came factor tables giving miles per minute (old-timers may recall Al Wintringham's "Argue-Not") or minutes per mile. About the same time, several kinds of TSD disc calculators came on the market: Blackwell's, the Marschalk, the Stevens, the Taylor. They helped somewhat. But since neither factor tables nor slide rules—linear, circular or spiral—could *accumulate* allowed running time, contestants' car cockpits continued to proliferate paper and profanity.

A quantum improvement came in the late 1950s in the form of pre-added factors. *Larry Reid's Rally Tables* (subsequently expanded, recomputed, and republished as *Larry Reid's New Rally Tables*, TAB No. 2014) lightened the navigator's burden considerably by providing worked-out running times for a generous range of speeds and distances. If navigating with tables gets a mite complicated at mid-leg speed-change points, large numbers of practitioners have trophies proving that it can be done.

In the meantime some ingenious, if not exceptionally efficient, special-purpose rally calculators appeared. The early homemade gadgets, some of which would have amazed Rube Goldberg, gave rise to the first commercially produced one, the Halda Speedpilot, the heart of which was a mechanical integrator—a variable-speed drive of limited precision. Presently the invention of the transistor and the development of integrated electronic circuits and miniaturized circuitry made it possible to squeeze incredibly accurate and versatile rally navigating machines into very small packages. The precision of these devices was matched by that of electric distance counters reading to the hundredth of a mile; and the ubiquitous curse of odometer "error" was exorcized by adjustable odometer drives—if you could afford the price.

Automatic—that is to say speedometer-cable-actuated—rally calculators such as the RoBo, the Tommy Box and the Zeron, to mention only a few, will do virtually everything but point you down the right road. They are not the sort of device, however, that you can unbuckle from under the dashboard, bring into the house and use to reconcile your bank statement or audit a supermarket cash register tape. The single-purpose nature of these machines—and their cost—have led many rallyists to seek less expensive solutions.

Of the portable mechanical calculators that were found to be adaptable to rally work, the most popular for many years was the Curta, and deservedly so. Although far from ideal as an adding/subtracting machine (the numbers had to be entered by positioning sliding buttons rather than by pressing keys), it performed multiplication and division rapidly enough. Looking for all the world like a pepper grinder, it was a tiny but capable adaptation of such carriage-shifting desk calculators as the Monroe. Like the Monroe and other office machines of that sort, the Curta provided two readouts, one showing how many times you had turned the crank, the other displaying the answer to the problem. Cranking up the minutes-per-mile factor so that the indicating dial matched the car odometer reading gave the allowed time for that distance, at that speed, in the answer dial. The beauty of the Curta for rallying lay in its ability to accumulate and store numbers; the speed factor could be changed at any time without disturbing the latest answer. Speed changes were therefore no fuss, and neither were pauses and gain-time operations. Indeed, with a Curta you could run a whole rally leg between scoring checkpoints using one odometer and one watch or clock without having to adjust or reset either of them.

Alas, the Curta fell victim to the phenomenal proliferation of inexpensive pocket electronic calculators in the early 1970s, which forced Contina Ltd. in Vaduz, Liechtenstein, to concede that the hand-crank was no match for the pushbutton-controlled electronic circuit. But if rallyists expected the first crop or two of pocket calculators to replace the Curta as the nearly ideal aid to navigation, their hopes were shattered when they discovered that these new electronic wonders of the age weren't up to the job. They would perform a chain of complex computations and give instantaneous answers. They would not, however, increment and store, increment and store...for the simple reason that they had no memory. At the first mid-leg change of speed the calculator—and the odometer and the timepiece—had to be started all over again from zero.

Although the single-memory pocket calculators offered more utility and could conceivably be used to accumulate, display and store time factors, they turned out to be markedly less than ideal, the principal reason being that they had no way of keeping account of, or displaying, the accumulated distance.

At that impasse the situation rested for some time. Then a fresh generation of pocket calculators with dramatically enhanced capabilities (and with some startling price tags) was born—machines conceived for use in such specialized fields as science and engineering, business and finance. Before long, many of these computing functions were combined in single multipurpose models boasting several memories and, to properly ice the cake, programmability. Moreover, as research and development costs were recovered and calculator sales boomed, the prices of these greatly advanced models dropped again and again. Best of all for rallyists, calculators of this kind form the basis of an average-speed navigation system so accurate, efficient and convenient that it is hard to imagine a better way.

This book, then, is devoted to demonstrating how two similar but different programmable pocket calculators can be employed not only in rally navigation but in rally scoring as well. They are the Hewlett-Packard HP-25 and the Texas Instruments SR-56. Either one will do the job beautifully. They are not, of course, the only programmables on the market, but each is typical of the broad class to which it belongs. The HP-25 uses the arithmetical system called Reverse Polish Notation; the SR-56 uses Algebraic Notation. The calculator programs in this book that are written for the HP-25 should be readily adaptable to any other RPN programmable model or make; and those written for the SR-56 should be easily adapted to any other AN programmable.

The HP-25 weighs six ounces and has eight addressable memories and forty-nine program steps. The SR-56 weighs eight and a half ounces and has ten addressable memories and one hundred program steps. The two have many similarities and many differences, but one thing they have in common is phenomenal computing power.

Are these programmables more calculator than you need for ordinary purposes? Possibly. On the other hand the Curta, apart from its singular usefulness in rally navigation, was *less* calculator than most of its users would have liked—and the HP-25 (and its companion piece the continuous-memory HP-25C) and the SR-56, even in these times of inflation, cost less. So even if you have no pressing need to solve problems in trigonometry, to convert rectangular/polar coordinates, to calculate mortgage amortizations or to find statistical means and standard deviations, they justify their price simply as rally instruments. And in odd moments when you have nothing better to do you can always engage them in a friendly game of Nimb or Lunar Lander Simulator.

Larry Reid

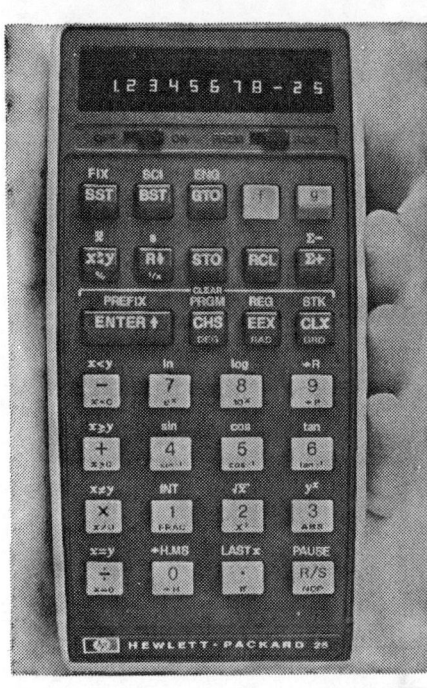

THE HEWLETT-PACKARD HP-25 PROGRAMMABLE POCKET ELECTRONIC CALCULATOR

AUTOMATIC MEMORY STACK

T
Z
Y
X

LAST X

STORAGE REGISTERS

R0
R1
R2
R3
R4
R5
R6
R7

THE HP-25 STORAGE REGISTERS

PROGRAM MEMORY

STEP 00
STEP 01
STEP 02
STEP 03

STEP 46
STEP 47
STEP 48
STEP 49

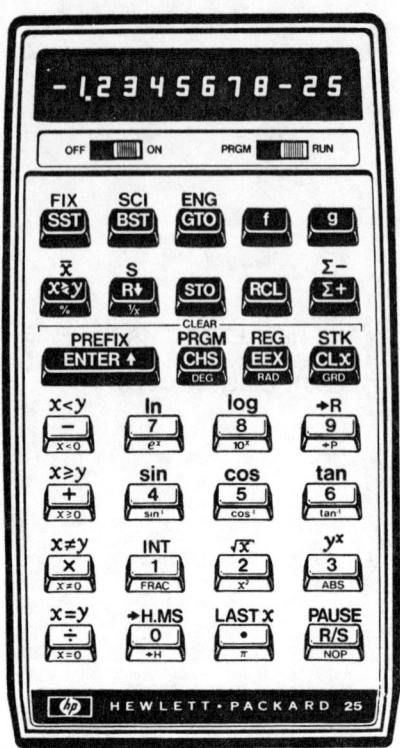

THE HP-25 KEYBOARD
The principal function of each key is printed in white or black on the key's flat face. Supplementary "gold" functions, enabled by the f key, are printed in gold above the keys; "blue" functions, enabled by the g key, are printed in blue on the keys' slanted front surface.

HEUER SEBRING

HEUER MONTE-CARLO

Seven-jewel stopclocks like these, designed for dashboard mounting, are excellent for rally work. Both record elapsed time to 1/5 second and 1/100 minute, have a time-out feature and are protected against accidental zeroing. The Sebring registers to 60 minutes and has a second second-hand for split-action timing. The Monte Carlo's jumping hour disc shows 0 – 12 hours.

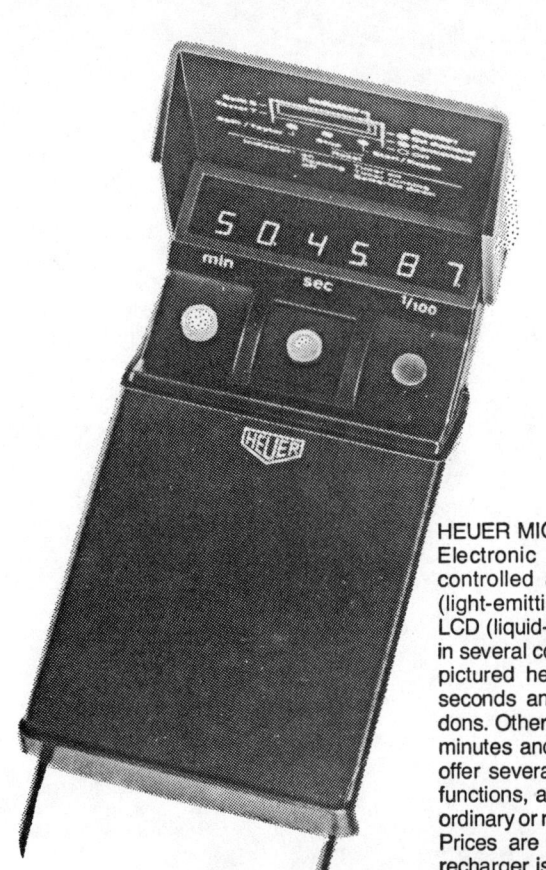

HEUER MICROSPLIT TIMER
Electronic stopwatches, quartz controlled and with either LED (light-emitting diode) display or LCD (liquid-crystal display), come in several configurations. The one pictured here reads in minutes, seconds and hundredths of seconds. Other models read in hours, minutes and decimal minutes. All offer several simultaneous timing functions, and all are powered by ordinary or rechargeable batteries. Prices are under $100; 110-volt recharger is less than $10 extra.

HALDA "TRIPMASTER" ODOMETER
When the three-position selector knob is turned to +, this mechanical mileage counter registers distance to 999.99 miles. With the knob at −, distance driven is subtracted. The 0 + off − position is handy aftergoing off course for turning around without adding distance while backing the car. The 0 button at right zeros the counter instantly; just above it, the protruding knob is for advancing or turning back the counter manually.

Part I
The Hewlett-Packard HP-25 Programmable Pocket Calculator

Chapter 1
Getting Acquainted with the HP-25

WHAT IS a programmable calculator? Briefly, it is a calculator that can be made to execute *automatically* the sequence of individual steps needed to be performed in the course of solving an arithmetical problem. If you can solve a problem using the calculator manually, you can program the calculator to solve the same problem, or a whole series of similar ones, at the press of the run/stop button. Indeed, repetitive calculations are what programmable calculators do best. The time-speed-distance problem, which has to be solved dozens, perhaps hundreds, of times during a rally, is typical. Having stored the navigational program, you key in the distance for which you want the allowed driving time (corrected for odometer error, of course), punch the run/stop button—and seconds later out comes the answer.

You aren't a computer programmer, you say? No matter; you don't have to be. You don't have to know anything about computer theory. You don't have to learn a computer language. The HP-25 is programmed through its keyboard. Having switched it to "program" mode, you press, in sequence, the keys just as if you were solving the problem manually. The calculator remembers these operations and, when you switch to "run" mode and hit the run/stop key, it automatically "presses" (internally) the same keys in the same sequence. As soon as it has solved the problem, it stops, displays the answer and is ready to go again using any different numbers that you want to key in.

Another iterative rally problem is the scoring—but let's not get ahead of ourselves....

The Keyboard

A new owner's first impression of the HP-25 is that it has a rather large and perhaps bewildering number of keys. There are in fact 30 keys, most of which serve more than one purpose. Twenty-one are three-function keys; five have two functions; only four are limited to one function. To utilize the function printed on the flat face of a key, you merely press the key. To select the function printed in gold above the key, first press the gold f key, then press the function key. To select the function printed in blue on the lower slanted face of a key, press the blue g key, then the function key. For example, to place the number 2 in the calculator, press the 2 key. To find the square root of the number shown in the display, press the f key, then press the key labeled, in gold, $\sqrt{x}$—the 2 key. To square the number displayed, press the g key, then the key with x^2 on its slanted face—again the 2 key.

If it were not for its multifunction keys, the HP-25 would have to have some *seventy* keys.

For purposes that will become evident later on, the keys are identified by keycodes, most of which are based on a simple matrix system in which the first digit of the code designates the horizontal row where the key is located, and the second digit designates the position of the key in that row. The rows are counted 1–7 from the top; the keys are counted 1–4 or 1–5 from left to right. For example, the f key's keycode is 14 (row 1, key 4); the ÷ key's keycode is 71. The ten keys that are not matrix coded are the number keys 0–9; their codes are 00, 01, . . . 09. Note that the keycodes pertain merely to key locations, not to key functions.

The 70-odd key functions of the HP-25 endow it with astounding power—so much power, in fact, that the straightforward calculations needed for rally navigation do not begin to test its amazing capabilities. In truth, it is not the computing power you need so much as those eight lovely memories. Nevertheless, we will review the basic functions of all the keys. The keys are designated here by their keycodes, and an asterisk indicates that the function is unlikely to be used in rally work.

11 (gold) FIX *Fix display*   Pressing f, then FIX, then a number key from 0–9 fixes the number of decimal points to be displayed.

The value is always rounded automatically in the last place displayed; however, the calculator always *computes* using the full complement of up to ten digits. For example, with the fixed-point notation at 2, π (pi) will be displayed as 3.14, but the value in the calculator is actually 3.141592654. To see for yourself, press g π f FIX 9.

11 SST *Single step* With the calculator in *program mode*, repeatedly pressing this key reviews the entered program step by step, displaying the number (00–49) and the contents of the next program step.

In *automatic run mode*, pressing this key displays the number and the keycode of the current program step; releasing the key causes the instruction to be executed and the result to be displayed, and moves to the next step. Thus you can review the actual working of a program in slow motion.

12 (gold) SCI* *Display scientific notation* For working with very large or very small numbers, scientific notation expresses a number as a mantissa of up to eight digits followed by an exponent (positive or negative) of 10. For example, the number 1234567 in scientific notation to seven decimal places is 1.2345670 06, meaning 1.2345670×10^6. Pressing f SCI followed by a number key from 0 to 7 fixes the number of places to be displayed.

12 BST *Back step* In *program mode*, displays the step number and the contents of the preceding program step.

In *automatic run mode*, pressing this key displays the step number and the keycode of the preceding program step; releasing it displays the original contents of the x-register. (The x-, y-, z- and t-registers will be taken up later.)

13 (gold) ENG* *Display engineering notation* Pressing f ENG followed by a number key from 0 to 5 expresses and displays numbers with exponents of 10 in multiples of 3 (0.000012345 becomes 12.345×10^{-6}; 99,000 becomes 99×10^3; etc.).

13 GTO *Go to* (followed by a two-digit program step number from 00–49):

In automatic run mode, positions the calculator to the program step of that number.

As a program instruction, permits program branching by causing the calculator to go to the program step specified. (We shall see later that program branching may be conditional or unconditional.)

14 f *Gold prefix key* This key must be pressed to call up a key's gold function.

15 g *Blue prefix key* This key must be pressed to call up a key's blue function.

21 $\overline{x}$* (gold) *Mean* Calculates the average of the numbers totaled by $\Sigma+$ in memory storage register 7. Used in statistical calculations.

21 $x{\rightleftarrows}y$ *x−y exchange* Exchanges the contents of the x- and y-registers; used principally to invert fractions.

21 (blue) *% Percent* Calculates x percent of y. When followed by $+$, $-$, $\times$ or $\div$, will add the answer to y, subtract the answer from y, multiply y by the answer or divide y by the answer.

22 (gold) s* *Standard deviation* Calculates standard deviation in statistical work.

22 R↓ *Roll down* Rolls down, in turn, the contents of the y-, z- and t-registers for display in the x-register.

22 (blue) *1/x Reciprocal* Calculates the reciprocal of the number displayed (divides 1 by that number).

23 STO *Store in memory* (followed by a number key from 0 to 7) stores the displayed number in the memory register specified. (The calculator has eight addressable memories, numbered 0–7.)

STO followed by an arithmetical operator key ($+$, $-$, $\times$, $\div$) performs arithmetic on the contents of the designated memory register: STO $+$ 1 adds the number in the x-register to the contents of memory 1; STO $-$ 1 subtracts the number in the x-register from the contents of memory 1; STO $\times$ 1 multiplies the contents of memory 1 by the number in the x-register; STO $\div$ 1 divides the contents of memory 1 by the number in the x-register. (The number in the x-register—which is always the number displayed—remains unchanged.)

24 RCL *Recall* (followed by a number key from 0 to 7) recalls the contents of the memory register specified and displays that value in the x-register (The value in the memory remains unchanged in the memory.)

25 (gold) $\Sigma-$* *Summation minus* Used in statistical work.

25 $\Sigma+$* *Summation plus* Used in statistical work.

31 (gold) CLEAR PREFIX *Clear prefix* is a correction key. If you have pressed *f*, *g*, STO, RCL or GTO by mistake, pressing *f* PREFIX will cancel that key.

31 ENTER *Enter* Pressing this key once copies the number displayed in the x-register into the y-register, opening the x-register

to receive another number that is to be keyed in in a two-function arithmetic operation; it serves to separate the first number from the one to follow, such separation being necessary in a calculator using Reverse Polish Notation (more about that later) rather than the more common algebraic notation.

Pressing ENTER twice copies the number into the z-register as well, and pressing the same key again copies it into the t-register as well.

32 (gold) CLEAR PRGM *Clear program* In *program mode* clears the program memory completely.

In *program run mode* resets the calculator to resume operating at program step 00.

32 CHS *Change sign* Changes the sign of the number displayed in the x-register from + to − or from − to +.

32 (blue) DEG* *Degrees* Used only in trigonometric calculations.

33 (gold) CLEAR REG *Clear registers* Replaces the contents of all eight memory storage registers with zeros.

(To clear a particular memory, press 0 STO followed by the number key corresponding to the number of the memory to be cleared.)

33 EEX *Enter exponent* The next numbers keyed in are exponents of 10. Used for working with very large or very small numbers.

33 (blue) RAD* *Radians* Used only in trigonometric calculations.

34 (gold) CLEAR STK *Clear stack* Clears the contents of the x-, y-, z- and t-registers.

34 (blue) CLx *Clear x* Clears the x-register, replacing the displayed number with zero.

34 (blue) GRD* *Grads* Used only in trigonometric calculations.

41 (gold) $x<y$ *If x is less than y . . .* A conditional test used in program branching.

41 − *Minus* Subtracts the number in the x-register from the number in the y-register.

41 (blue) $x<0$ *If x is less than zero . . .* A conditional test used in program branching.

07 (gold) ln* *Natural logarithm* Computes log to the base e of the number in the x-register.

07 (blue) e^x* *Natural antilogarithm*   Raises e to the power of the number in the x-register.

08 (gold) log* *Common logarithm*   Computes the log to the base 10 of the number in the x-register.

08 (blue) 10^x* *Common antilogarithm*   Raises 10 to the power of the number in the x-register.

09 (gold) →R* *Rectangular coordinate conversion*   Strictly for the engineering fraternity.

09 (blue) →P* *Polar coordinate conversion*   Ditto.

51 (gold) $x \geq y$ *If x is equal to or greater than y* . . .   A conditional test used in program branching.

51 + *Plus*   Adds the number in the x-register to the number in the y-register.

51 (blue) $x \geq 0$ *If x is equal to or greater than 0*. . .Another conditional test.

04 (gold) sin* *Sine*   A trig function.

04 (blue) $\sin^{-1}$* *Arc sine*   A trig function.

05 (gold) cos* *Cosine*   A trig function.

05 (blue) $\cos^{-1}$* *Arc cosine*   A trig function.

06 (gold) tan* *Tangent* A trig function.

06 (blue) $\tan^{-1}$* *Arc Tangent* A trig function

61 (gold) $x \neq y$ *If x is unequal to y* . . .   Another conditional test for program branching.

61 × *Times*   Multiplies the number in the y-register by the number in the x-register.

61 (blue) $x \neq 0$ *If x is unequal to zero* . . .   Another conditional test for program branching.

01 (gold) INT* *Integer*   Leaves only the integer portion (left of the decimal point) of the number in the x-register.

01 (blue) FRAC* *Fraction*   Leaves only the fractional portion (right of the decimal point) of the number in the x-register.

02 (gold) $\sqrt{x}$* *Square root*   Calculates the square root of the number in the x-register.

02 (blue) x^2* *Square*   Calculates the square of the number in the x-register.

03 (gold) y^x* *Power* Raises the number in the y-register to the power of the number in the x-register. (The power can be positive, negative or a fraction.)

03 (blue) ABS**Absolute*   Gives the absolute (positive) value of the number in the x-register, whether the number is negative or positive.

71 (gold) $x = y$ *If x equals y* . . .   Another conditional test.

71 ÷ *Divide*   Divides the number in the y-register by the number in the x-register.

71 (blue) $x = 0$ *If x is equal to zero* . . .   Another conditional test.

00 (gold)→H.MS *Hours, minutes, seconds*   Converts displayed decimal hours (or degrees) to hours, minutes and seconds (or degrees, minutes and seconds).

00 (blue)→H *Hours*   Converts displayed hours-minutes-seconds (or degrees-minutes-seconds) value to decimal hours (or decimal degrees).

73 (gold) LASTx *Recall last x*   Recalls and displays the number previously displayed in the x-register.

73   .   *Decimal*   Enters decimal point.

73 (blue) π* *Pi*   Places the value of pi (to nine decimal places) in the x-register.

74 (gold) PAUSE *Pause to display*   *In the automatic run mode*, interrupts the program for about one second, displays the contents of the x-register, then resumes execution of the program. If a longer display is desired, one or more additional f PAUSE instructions may be entered in the program at this point.

74 R/S *Run/stop*   *In run mode*, if pressed from the keyboard, begins execution of a stored program, or stops execution if the program is running. *As a program instruction* it halts program execution.

74 (blue) NOP *No operation*   *In automatic run mode*, causes the calculator to execute no operation at this step and to continue executing the program with the next program step. This is essentially a program-correction key.

Keys 00–09, when used unprefixed by f or g, are of course digit keys for entering the numbers 0–9.

The Switches

At the very top of the keyboard, the ON-OFF switch controls the power supply. Whether the calculator is plugged into the charger or not, switching to ON displays 0.00, signifying that the calculator is ready to use. The PRGM-RUN switch is set to PRGM only when a program is to be entered; it will display 00, indicating that the calculator is ready to receive program step 01. The switch is set to RUN when a program is to be run or when the calculator is to be used for conventional manual operation. Note that when a program has been entered, the calculator can still be used for manual operations. (Such operations, however, should not disturb the contents of any memory being used in the program.) The program will remain stored and available as long as the power switch is left in the ON position; switching the power OFF will kill the program and clear all the other memory registers as well.

The Registers

Being now familiar with the externals of the HP-25, you will want to learn something about its innards. Inside the calculator are 62 boxes, which when the power switch is first turned ON are always empty. There are four sets of these boxes, all called registers. The automatic memory "stack" has four registers—x, y, z and t; the memory bank has eight—0–7; and the program memory has fifty—00–49—of which forty-nine will store automatic-program commands. The single "last x" register always contains the value previously displayed. The diagram shown in the front of the book will help you to visualize these various storage registers.

All the registers serve to receive and store data of one kind or another. Each set of registers works in its own particular fashion.

The Automatic Memory Stack

The function of the four-register "stack" is to store intermediate numbers and results needed to complete a calculation. Each such number occupies one "box," or register, and the numbers are moved automatically up and down the stack from one box to another as the occasion requires. It is in the stack that the calculator does most of its calculating (the exception is where arithmetic is performed in the memories, and even there the stack is involved); and this automatic stacking feature accounts for much of the HP-25's ability to solve long and complex equations with ease.

Henceforth in this book the four stack registers—the x-, y-, z- and t-registers—will be referred to as R_x, R_y, R_z and R_t.

The operation of the stack, although not terribly complicated, is a bit hard to visualize unless you have an HP-25 in your hands. Since this book is not intended as a comprehensive treatise on the internal workings of the calculator, no effort will be made here to explain in detail the operation of the stack (to which the Owner's Handbook devotes thirteen pages); the stack's important aspects for our purposes are these:

1. The display is *always* the contents of R_x.
2. The first number (a number may be one or many digits) to be keyed in goes into R_x and is displayed. Pressing the ENTER key will then copy that number into R_y and, although the number is still displayed as the contents of R_x, prepares R_x to receive a new number. When a new number is keyed in, it goes into R_x and is displayed, the first number remaining in R_y. One function of the stack, then, is to separate consecutive number entries.
3. The number in R_x is always the operant value in any calculation. In other words, it is always the x value that is added to or subtracted from the y value; it is always the x value by which a y value is multiplied or divided; and in exponential calculations it is the xth power to which y is raised and the xth root of y that is extracted. Similarly, when arithmetic is performed in any of the eight memory storage registers, it is always x that is added to or subtracted from the contents of the memory, and always x by which the value in the memory is multiplied or divided.
4. You can inspect the contents of the four stack registers by pressing R↓ to "roll down" the y, z and t values into the R_x display. Pressing R↓ four times restores the values to their respective locations in the stack.
5. You can clear the entire stack at any time by pressing f STK.

The Memory Storage Registers

The eight memory storage registers, which are independent of the stack, provide for storing numbers that may be required as constants or as parts of later calculations. They can be addressed manually or as elements of an automatic program. The numbers they are storing can be recalled, and arithmetic can be performed on stored numbers without recalling them. From here on in this book the memory registers will be designated as R_0, R_1 and so on to R_7.

When a value is to be stored in a memory, that value must first appear in Rx. Then pressing STO followed by a number key from 0 to 7 copies the displayed value into the memory register of that number. (The value remains in R$_x$ and in the display.) For example, keying 98.76 STO 0 stores the value 98.76 in R$_0$.

To retrieve a stored number, press RCL, then the key corresponding to the number of the register address. RCL 3, for example, copies into R$_x$ the value in R$_3$, even if that value happens to be zero. In the retrieval process the value is not removed from the memory; it is merely borrowed—copied into R$_x$ and displayed. The stored value remains in the memory until it is either overwritten by a new STO instruction or cleared. You can clear Rn (n being the register address) by pressing 0 STOn, overwriting the new value 0. To clear all eight registers, press f REG. Switching the calculator OFF also clears all the memory registers.

Storage-Register Arithmetic

Arithmetical operations can be performed on the contents of the memory registers in these ways:

Pressing keys STO + n adds the value in R$_x$ to the value in R$_n$.
Pressing STO − n subtracts the value in R$_x$ from the value in R$_n$.
Pressing STO × n multiplies the value in R$_n$ by the value in R$_x$.
Pressing STO ÷ n divides the value in R$_n$ by the value in R$_x$.

The HP-25's ability to do arithmetic in the memories enhances its power considerably; you will find it an important part of the rally navigation programs.

The Program-Step Register

The automatic-program memory provides 50 boxes, 49 of which are available to store program instructions. These registers are numbered in double digits, R$_{00}$ − R$_{49}$, and they must always be addressed in that manner. Step 00 will not store a program instruction, being reserved for "initializing" the program; the program steps are memorized in registers R$_{01}$ − R$_{49}$.

You write a program, step by step, into the program registers just as you would press the keys if you were solving the problem manually. Program steps are entered with the calculator in *program mode*—with the PRGM-RUN switch set at PRGM. Then any *data entries* (more about these later) are entered in *run mode*. That done, pressing *f* PRGM sets the calculator to program step 00, and pressing R/S (run/stop) starts the running of the program.

Programming the HP-25 is explained in some detail in Chapter 3.

The Last-x Register

The LASTx register is a separate automatic register that preserves the value that was in R_x before the most recent function was performed. To recall the contents of this register into R_x press *f* LASTx.

The ability to retrieve the previous x saves having to key it in again and so is useful not only in calculations where the value recurs, but also in correcting certain keyboard errors.

Reverse Polish Notation

If you have ever used any ordinary pocket calculator (or even an extraordinary one), you can hardly have failed to notice something about the HP-25 keyboard that differentiates it from most of the others. Where, you may have been wondering, is the "equals" key? The answer is that there is none. And the reason it is omitted is that it is not needed.

Most pocket calculators, as you undoubtedly know, are designed to work with a sequence of keystrokes based on *algebraic notation*. Under this system you press the keys in the same order as you would write the problem on paper: $5 + 3 = ?$ $5 - 3 = 0$ $5 \times 3 = ?$ $5 \div 3 = ?$ The answer lights up in the display when the = key is pressed. It is a sensible, straightforward, serviceable system, easy to learn, remember and use—to a degree.

AN turns out to have certain limitations where complex (and sometimes not so complex) equations are concerned. Consider how you would solve this one using a basic, memoryless pocket calculator:

$$\frac{(2 \times 3) + (4 \times 5)}{(6 \times 7)} = ?$$

You would have to work it out on the installment plan, so to speak. First you would multiply 2×3 and make a note of the answer, 6. Then you would multiply 4×5, getting 20, and add that to 6, getting 26. Then you would multiply 6 × 7, getting 42. Finally you would divide 26 by 42 to get the answer, 0.619047619. The keystrokes would be these:

2 × 3 = (intermediate answer: 6; make a note)
4 × 5 = (intermediate answer: 20)
+ 6 = (intermediate answer: 26; make a note)
6 × 7 = (intermediate answer: 42; make a note)
26 ÷ 42 = (at last, the answer, 0.6190476)

You have made 21 keystrokes and three written notes.

Now graduate to a one-memory calculator with an $x \leqq y$ exchange:

2 × 3 = M+ (6 stored in memory)
4 × 5 = M+ (26 stored in memory)
6 × 7 = 42 (in display)
$x \leqq y$ ÷ RM = (answer in display)

That took 18 keystrokes. Note that if the calculator had no exchange key you would have had to make a note along the way or else start off by working on the denominator instead of the numerator of the fraction.

A more sophisticated AN calculator, one that has parenthesis keys and the ability to set off parenthetical terms of an expression, will do the job in a continuous operation that need not be interrupted for notetaking—but you must be wary about "solving the problem just as it is written"...

Using the Texas Instruments SR-56 programmable calculator that is the subject of Part II of this book, if you keyed in the equation as it is written you would get a wrong answer:
(2 × 3) + (4 × 5) ÷ (6 × 7) = would give 6.476190476, which turns out to be

$$6 + \left(\frac{4 \times 5}{6 \times 7}\right)$$

To get the right answer, you must set up the equation in one of two other ways. One is this:

(2 × 3) + (4 × 5) = ÷ (6 × 7) =

The other:

((2 × 3) + (4 × 5)) ÷ (6 × 7) =

In the first case you have taken an intermediate total (at the first =) and used 18 keystrokes; in the second you have encased the entire numerator in double parentheses and expended 19 keystrokes.

Any thoughtful arithmetical semanticist will contend, rightly enough, that the horizontal line separating the numerator from the denominator of a fraction is equivalent to a pair of parentheses enclosing the entire numerator and a corresponding pair enclosing the entire denominator. All true and all very well, so long as you understand what the ground rules really are.

Now see how the HP-25 handles $\dfrac{(2 \times 3) + (4 \times 5)}{(6 \times 7)} = ?$

2 ENTER 3×
4 ENTER 5 ×
+
6 ENTER 7 ×
÷

We have pared the keystrokes to 14, and that is good. Better yet, we have not had to key in any add-to-memory or retrieve-from-memory commands, nor have we had to make notes of intermediate answers. Best of all, we have not had to subject the equation to sharp scrutiny or deep analysis, nor have we supplied any more parentheses than we started out with. The calculator has automatically stored the intermediate results in the automatic stack and has brought them back into play as they were needed.

The name given to this method of producing intermediate answers as soon as an arithmetical function key (+, − , ×, ÷ and others) is pressed is Reverse Polish Notation. The manifold virtues of RPN logic will impress you after you have had a little practice using it. It enables you to work with just one function at a time. It displays intermediate results as soon as it calculates them, allowing you to check each step in a computation as you go along. It stores the intermediate results for you automatically and recalls them when they are needed, all without having to be told to do so. It allows you, in sum, to calculate not as you would *write* the problem but as you would *solve* it. These advantages become even more impressive when you get into programming the HP-25.

Although RPN obviates the need for an "equals" key, it does require a means of separating two or more numbers that are to be keyed in consecutively. This separation is accomplished by the ENTER key. If you wish to add 3 + 5, you press 3 ENTER 5 +. Pressing 3 places 3 in R_x; ENTER copies 3 into R_y, and although 3 remains displayed as the contents of R_x, the x-register is now prepared to receive the next number, 5. Pressing 5 overwrites the displayed 3, and pressing + adds the value in R_x (5) to that in R_y (3), displaying the sum (8) and, incidentally, clearing R_y. *Now* if you want to key in a new number, it is not necessary to press ENTER. Whenever any value in the display got there as a result of a function operation (in this case the operation was an addition), R_x automatically readies itself to receive another keyed-in value; ENTER is required only when you are introducing two number values by keying them in consecutively.

The ENTER key can be pressed once or twice or more when you want to raise the value in R_y higher in the stack for retrieval later. This multiple ENTER routine is of no concern in rally navigation, but it greatly simplifies rally scoring programs, which are treated in a later chapter.

The Display

Turning the power switch ON with the selector switch at RUN immediately displays 0.00, the contents of R_x. As numbers are keyed in, they appear in sequence from left to right. In the course of operation, all numbers are displayed as they are keyed in, and all intermediate and final answers are shown as they are calculated.

The display accommodates ten digits. Normally, a number is shown to two decimal places. As noted earlier, the number of decimal places to be displayed can be fixed from none to nine; but no matter how many (or how few) places are fixed, when you key in a value with decimal digits all the digits are displayed.

In RUN mode the value displayed is always the value in R_x.

In PRGM mode the display shows up to eight digits. The first two are the number of the program step just entered; the others are the keycode of that step.

The Power Supply

There are actually two models of the HP-25 calculator: the original, now designated the HP-25A, and the HP-25C, the "C" denoting "continuous memory." Both are powered by a rechargeable battery pack. The pack is replaceable, but it need not be removed from the calculator for recharging. The calculator can be used while connected through the charging unit (included in this calculator kit) to a 110- or 220-volt AC source. When it is run on the batteries only, a fully charged pack will provide from two to five hours' operating time. When the pack needs recharging, the calculator display gives warning by showing all the decimal points except the correct one. Recharging time is six hours.

Since switching the power off kills the contents of all the HP-25A's storage registers, the program memories included, navigators will generally leave the power switch on all through a rally, or at least throughout each major section; and since most rallies last longer than two hours and many last longer than five, the question of calculator power resources arises.

There are ready answers. One solution is to buy a reserve power pack; it consists of a spare battery pack and an attachment that lets you charge it outside the calculator and carry it along as a replacement. The cost is about $20.

Another solution, which will cost about the same, is to buy from an automotive supply store a 12VDC – 110VAC converter of the type that is commonly used to operate electric shavers and other low-wattage appliances. The cords of such converters plug into the car's cigarette lighter socket. Plug the HP charger into the converter and the calculator cord into the charger, and let your car battery provide the power. (Be sure that the lighter circuit does not run through the ignition switch. If it does, rewire it to a terminal that is fed directly from the car battery, such as an electric clock terminal.) The typical shaver converter is a 15-watt unit and will easily meet the demand of the HP 5-watt charger.*

When running the calculator on its batteries you can conserve the charge by limiting the lighted display when the power is left on between calculations by keying in the number 1. The display uses much more current than do the electronic calculating circuits, and the digit 1, which illuminates only two elements of one seven-element display, imposes the least current drain.

---

*As this was written, Hewlett-Packard was developing a 12-volt recharger designed specifically for use in automobiles, boats and aircraft. Estimated price: $25 or $30.

Another answer to the question of how to stretch the power supply is the HP-25C. This model differs from the HP-25 A in only one respect: When you turn off the HP-25C, it preserves the information stored in the eight addressable memories, in the 49-step program register and in the LASTx register. If left turned off, it will retain these data for up to a month and a half. (The battery pack must be left in the calculator.) When switched on again, it will go automatically to program step 00. (Although the numbers in the stack—R_x, R_y, R_z and R_t—are not retained, the value in R_x can be saved if you press + or − before switching off; later you can retrieve that number by pressing f LASTx.)

The standby power being only 1/80,000 of the normal operating power (5 microwatts vs. 400 milliwatts), switching off the HP-25C when it is not being used to perform calculations or to run programs will markedly lessen the rate of battery drain. And if you do have to substitute a fresh battery pack, a capacitor saves the stored data long enough to let you effect the change.

Yes, the HP-25C costs more than the HP-25A. Whether it is the one for you depends on the kinds of rallies you enter—how long they last, how often you participate. In any event (look on that as a pun if you wish) both HP-25 models are programmed and operated in the same way.

Calculating with the HP-25

If you are accustomed to using an algebraic-notation pocket calculator, you may need a little time to get used to the sequence of keystrokes required by Reverse Polish Notation. Two or three minutes should suffice. Here are some typical basic calculations as performed by the HP-25:

$$12 + 34 = ?$$
Keystrokes: 1 2 ENTER 3 4 +98 − 76 =?

Keystrokes: 9 8 ENTER 7 6 − 45 × 56 =?

Keystrokes: 4 5 ENTER 5 6 × 45 ÷ 56 =?

Keystrokes: 4 5 ENTER 5 6 ÷

Chain calculations will easily solve more complex expressions. For instance:

$$\frac{(12 + 34) \times (98 - 76)}{(45 \div 56)} = ?$$

Keystrokes:	12 ENTER 34 +	display: 46.00
	98 ENTER 76 −	display: 22.00
	×	display: 1012.00
	45 ENTER 56 ÷	display: 0.80
	÷	display: 1259.38

Although these sample calculations hardly begin to challenge the remarkable power of the HP-25, once you have learned to perform them you will be capable of handling any computation you are likely to encounter on a rally.

Chapter 2
Navigational Arithmetic

NAVIGATING WITH a pocket calculator brings nothing new to the arithmetic of time, speed and distance. The principles abide; only the mechanics of handling them are different. This chapter briefly reviews the principles and explains how the HP-25 manipulates the numbers with only a little help from you.

The Time-Speed-Distance Equation

The equation $D = R \times T$ (*distance* equals *speed* multiplied by *time*) and its corollaries $R = D \div T$ and $T = D \div R$ are the key to the average-speed problem in all its variations. When you know any two terms, solving for the unknown one is simple. Since rally distances are ordinarily measured in miles and car speeds in miles per hour (at this writing the United States has not gone metric), the equations are more usefully expressed thus:

$$miles = mph \times hours \qquad miles = \frac{mph \times minutes}{60}$$

$$miles = \frac{mph \times seconds}{3600}$$

$$mph = \frac{miles}{hours} \qquad mph = \frac{miles \times 60}{minutes}$$

$$mph = \frac{miles \times 3600}{seconds}$$

$$hours = \frac{miles}{mph} \qquad\qquad minutes = \frac{miles \times 60}{mph}$$

$$seconds = \frac{miles \times 3600}{mph}$$

If you already own an HP-25 try the following problems for practice; if not, these examples will show you how to handle them. The keystrokes are given first, followed by an explanation of what happens inside an RPN calculator.

(a) You are to drive for 8 minutes at 25.6 mph; what distance will you cover?

$$D = \frac{25.6 \times 8}{60}$$

(Power switch ON; selector switch at RUN.)

25.6	25.6 in R_x
ENTER	25.6 to R_y; R_x is ready for next number
8	8 in R_x
×	Multiplies y by x; 204.80 in R_x
60	60 in R_x; 204.80 in R_y
÷	Divides y by x and displays answer: 3.41 (miles)

(b) You have 45 minutes to drive 28 miles; what average speed must you maintain?

$$R = \frac{28 \times 60}{45}$$

28	28 in R_x
ENTER	28.00 to R_y; R_x is ready for next number
60	60 in R_x
×	Multiplies y by x; 1680.00 in R_x
45	45 in R_x; 1680.00 in R_y
÷	Divides y by x and displays answer: 37.33 (mph)

(c) You are to drive 37 1/2 miles at an average speed of 33 mph; how long will it take?

$$R = \frac{37.5}{33}$$

37.5	37.5 in R_x
ENTER	37.50 to R_y; R_x is ready for next number
33	33 in R_x
÷	Divides y by x and displays 1.14

This answer, 1.14 hours, seems not very useful. Press f FIX 4. Now you have 1.1364 hours. But what is that in clock time? To find out, press f H.MS. The display now shows 1.0811—1 hour 8 minutes 11 seconds. You desire more precision? Press f FIX 6 and get 1 hour 8 minutes 10.90 seconds. If you happen to own a copy of A NEW GUIDE TO RALLYING, look on page 82....

The Odometer Check

Unless you have never rallied before (in which case we unabashedly suggest that you rush out and buy the book just mentioned), you know that every average-speed rally begins with a run of ten miles or more to allow you to compare your odometer with the one that was used to officially measure the rally course. Once you know the "error" ("difference" is a purer term, but "odometer error" is firmly established in the vernacular of the sport), you can take steps to prevent the discrepancy from making you late or early at the scoring checkpoints. If your odometer reads higher than the official mileage at the end of the check, you will tend to arrive late at the checkpoints (a *l*ong reading = *l*ate); if it reads lower than the official mileage, you will tend to be early (a short reading = too soon). In addition, if a turn, a change of average speed or some other action is called for at some specified official distance from the start of a rally leg, you must be able to determine what that distance is according to *your* odometer.

The Correction Factors

Accordingly, at the end of the odometer check you have to calculate two correction factors; we will call them Factor A and Factor B and refer to them thus throughout this book.

Factor A is $\dfrac{\text{official distance}}{\text{odometer distance}}$ Factor B is $\dfrac{\text{odometer distance}}{\text{official distance}}$

The factors are used in several ways:

To convert odometer miles to official miles, multiply odometer miles by Factor A

To convert official miles to odometer miles, multiply official miles by Factor B.

To convert official speed to indicated speed, multiply official speed by Factor B.

To convert official minutes per mile to indicated minutes per mile, multiply official minutes per mile by Factor A.

Assume that at the end of an odometer check of 20.20 official miles your odometer reads 20.44. Then Factor A is 20.20 ÷ 20.44. Using the HP-25, the keystrokes are these:

20.2 ENTER 20.44 ÷

If you have not fixed the decimal point otherwise, the answer will be shown as 0.99. Now key in ƒ FIX 9. The full value of the factor displayed, 0.988258317, is what you will be using.

To get Factor B(20.44 ÷ 20.2) it is not necessary to reenter the two values. Factor B is the reciprocal of Factor A, and the calculator will figure Factor B for you in two additional keystrokes: *g* 1/*x* displays it instantly: 1.011881188. Neat, is it not?

Later, when we get into the fascinating business of programming the HP-25, you will see how the two factors, stored in two calculator memories, are drawn on to make the necessary correction computations automatically.

Special Problems

Even while a navigation program is stored, all of the calculator's many computing functions are available for auxiliary uses, except while the program is actually running and provided you do not disturb any of the memories needed by the program. Since rallies present many problems that have to be solved on the side, the HP-25's ability to play a dual role enhances its value inestimably.

The Average of the Averages

Consider this instruction:

Drive the first of the next section at 21.45 mph and the second half at 31.45 mph.

Not being told how long the section is, you have to find the average of the average speeds. You do *not* do this by adding 21.45 and 31.45 and dividing 52.9 by 2 to get 26.45 mph; the arithmetic of average speeds is not that simple. The average you need is the *harmonic mean*, and the equation is this:

$$\frac{2}{(1 \div 21.45) + (1 \div 31.45)}$$

As you will know from having studied your HP-25 Owner's Handbook—an outstanding piece of writing and printing—the keystrokes are these:

2 ENTER 1 ENTER 21.45 ÷ 1 ENTER 31.45 ÷ + ÷

The answer, 25.50482042 (press *f* FIX 9 to display the entire value), is the average speed to be entered in the rally program for this section.

Note that it is not necessary to reduce the slightly complex equation to its more simplified form, which is:

$$\frac{2\,(21.45 \times 31.45)}{21.45 + 31.45}$$

In A NEW GUIDE TO RALLYING on page 102 an "average of the averages" problem is given, along with the answer, but the method by which the solution is reached is left to the reader. Perhaps now is a good time to trace the steps and show how effortlessly the HP-25 performs them. The problem is this:

> Average 48 mph for the first half of the next leg; then change to a speed such that your average speed for the entire leg will be 36 mph.

Again you must calculate a harmonic mean. Calling on the equation $T = D/R$ and hypothesizing a leg distance of 2 miles, you can see that the time allowed to drive the whole leg, in hours, is 2/36. Similarly, the time to drive the first mile is 1/48 hour. Then the time left for the second mile is 2/36 − 1/48. Once you have calculated the time for the second mile, you can call on the formula $R = D/T$ to find the average speed for that mile. The equation to be solved, then, is:

$$R = \frac{1}{2/36 - 1/48}$$

The keystrokes:

1 ENTER 2 ENTER 36 ÷ 1 ENTER 48 ÷ − ÷

The answer is 28.80 mph for the second half of the leg. (Obviously, in this particular case the rallymaster would have to identify the half-way point for you somehow.)

For an interesting demonstration of the HP-25's intelligence try this one:

You have driven the first half of a trip at an average speed of 15 mph; what average speed must you maintain during the second half in order to average 30 mph for the whole trip?

The equation is:

$$1/x = 2/30 - 1/15$$

This time let's avail ourselves of the calculator's reciprocal function. The keystrokes are:

2 ENTER 30 ÷ 15 g 1/x − g 1/x

If you have recognized this ancient brain-teaser you will not be surprised when the calculator displays "Error," indicating that there is no solution. If you have used 4 minutes to drive 1 mile at 15 mph, and if driving 2 miles at 30 mph takes 4 minutes, then there is no way to average 30 mph for the 2 miles.

Analyzing Equations and Formulas

Nothing that has been said here in panegyrizing the HP-25 is meant to imply that this calculator—or any calculator—will do your thinking for you. It will do arithmetic for you, quickly and accurately; but it is up to you to analyze the problem and tell the calculator how to handle it. Often you will have to manipulate an expression before you can solve it; if it is a complex one, you will at least have to look it over carefully before attempting to feed it to the machine. Consider this equation (which, you may be glad to know, has nothing at all to do with rallying):

$$\sqrt{\frac{1 + (2 \times 3)(4 + 5)^2}{67 - (8 \div 9)}}$$

The general rule is to start with the innermost term and work outward, rather as though you were peeling an onion from the inside. Once you've acquired the knack, you'll find it not at all a tearful business. This is how it goes:

4 ENTER 5 + g x^2
2 ENTER 3 × X
1+   So much for the numerator . . .
67 ENTER
8 ENTER 9 ÷ −   and the denominator . . .
÷   and the complex fraction . . .
$f \sqrt{x}$ and finally the root, 2.71

Percentages

Ever hopeful of confusing you, rallymasters frequently give you instructions like these:

> Your average speed is 40 mph. At point A increase your average speed by 10 percent. At point B decrease your average speed by 10 percent.

Surely you will not let yourself be duped into changing speed from 40 to 44 and back to 40. Let the calculator do the job for you using the % key. The keystrokes are:

40 ENTER 10 g % +   First speed change is to 44.00
10 g % −   Final speed is 39.60

"Phantom Car" Problems

Another recurring favorite is the multifaceted "phantom car" gimmick, of which this is one version:

> At the instant you start this leg, a space-age phantom car exactly 600 miles up the road from you starts driving toward you at the speed of sound, which under today's atmospheric conditions has been determined as 1,100 feet per second. Your average speed is to be such that you will meet the phantom car after you have driven exactly 37.5 miles.

The formula for finding your average speed is

$$B = \frac{A \times D}{C - D}$$

where A = the speed of the phantom car in miles per hour
B = the speed of the rally car in miles per hour
C = the miles between the two cars at the start
D = the miles to be driven by the rally car to meet the phantom car

But the speed of the phantom car is given not in miles per hour; it is in feet per second. You have been warned that before using the calculator you often must use your head. This is one of those times, the question being how to convert 1,100 feet per second to miles per hour. There are, in fact, two approaches.

Your reasoning will tell you that 1100 ft/sec = 60 × 1100 ft/min = 60 × 60 × 1100 ft/hr, and that since there are 5280 feet in a mile the speed in miles per hour is (3600 × 1100) ÷ 5280. Key in 3600 ENTER 1100 × 5280 ÷ . There you have it, 750 mph.

Alternatively, you know surely that 60 mph = 88 ft/sec (5280 ÷ 60).* Then (1100 ÷ 88) × 60 gives the same result, the keystrokes being, of course, 1100 ENTER 88 ÷ 60 × .

Now that you know A in miles per hour, you can proceed to substitute the values of A, C and D in the equation:

$$B = \frac{750 \times 37.5}{600 - 37.5}$$

Try it on your HP-25. If you don't get 50 mph the first time, you need more practice. You did get it? Then have a go at this:

Two minutes before you start the next leg, a phantom car takes off from a position right beside you at an **average speed unknown to you.** Your average speed is 30 mph. You will overtake the phantom car after you have driven exactly 5 miles. At that point change your average speed to that of the phantom car.

You will find a promising formula on page 105 of A NEW GUIDE TO RALLYING;

$$A = \frac{B(D - C)}{D}$$

---

*Actually (5280 × 60) ÷ 3600.

where A = the speed of the phantom car in miles per hour
B = the speed of the rally car in miles per hour
C = the miles the phantom car is ahead at the start
D = the miles the rally car must travel to catch the phantom car

Ah, now you are faced with *two* unknowns, C as well as A. In order to find C, the distance the phantom car is ahead of you after having traveled for two minutes at speed A, you *will* have to get your brain in top gear.

Since you know that *miles* = (*mph* × *minutes*) ÷ 60, it is plain that the phantom car has traveled $(A \times 2) \div 60$ miles. Substitute this and the other known values in the equation:

$$A = \frac{30\,(5 - 2A/60)}{5}$$

Then $5A = 30\left(5 - \dfrac{2A}{60}\right) = 30\left(\dfrac{300 - 2A}{60}\right) = \dfrac{300 - 2A}{2}$;

and $10A = 300 - 2A$; $12A = 300$; $A = \dfrac{300}{12} = 25$

For once you did not need a calculator! If the numbers were much more complex, however, an equation like this could be difficult. For that reason the Appendix of this book lists a full set of phantom-car formulas that includes a general expression of this one, which, when E = the minutes the phantom car is ahead at the start, is:

$$A = \frac{60BD}{60D + BE}$$

If you had had this formula to begin with, it would have looked like this with the known values substituted:

$$A = \frac{60 \times 30 \times 5}{(60 \times 5) + (30 \times 2)}$$

Then the calculator keystrokes would have been:
60 ENTER 30 × 5 ×
60 ENTER 5 ×
30 ENTER 2 × + ÷

* * *

Although this may not be the place to argue matters of pedagogy, instructional methodology or educational philosophy, the foregoing exercise does seem to prove a point. It has been argued that schoolchildren with access to inexpensive pocket calculators are using them as crutches, learning how to push buttons instead of developing the mathematical sense that they will need all their lives. That contention, in this writer's opinion, is nonsense. No amount of button-pushing will give anyone the right answer to any mathematical problem unless he knows which buttons to push. Calculators eliminate much of the drudgery in arithmetic, but they cannot possibly substitute for understanding. With the drudgery largely removed, the road to understanding would seem not merely less arduous but infinitely more inviting.

Chapter 3
Programming the HP-25

YOU MAY HAVE heard that to be a computer programmer you must know all about computer theory, higher mathematics, computer languages and a great deal else. The extent to which that is true depends on the nature and magnitude of the operation. Programming the HP-25, however, is only as difficult as using the calculator to solve problems "manually," as we have been doing. In a word, if you can make the HP-25 solve a problem, you can, with only a little more ingenuity, program it to solve the same problem, using different numbers, over and over again as many times as you wish, literally at the press of a button. A program for the HP-25 consists essentially of the same series of keystrokes that you would use to solve the problem manually. Once you have stored the keystrokes in the automatic program memory, the calculator will run through them in sequence, automatically.

Program-Building

Let's spend some time on a typical routine that happens to have nothing whatsoever to do with rallying: converting a temperature from Fahrenheit to centigrade. The formula for the conversion is:

$$°C = (°F - 32) \times 5/9$$

Suppose that you want to change 98.6°F to degrees centigrade. The keystrokes are these:

98.6 ENTER	Places 98.6 in R_x and in R_y
32 −	Places 32 in R_x and subtracts $y - x$, displaying 66.60
5 ENTER	Places 5 in R_y and moves 66.6 up the stack into R_z
9 ÷	Divides 5 by 9 (y/x), displaying 0.56 in R_x
×	Multiplies 66.6 by 0.56 (xy) and displays the answer: 37.00 (degrees C)

No problem, you may say. Right. But now suppose that the outdoor temperature is a balmy 80°F and you want the Centigrade equivalent. You go through the same routine with a new number: 80 ENTER 32 − 5 ENTER 9 ÷ × . If you have still another temperature to convert, you will have to repeat the process. Clearly, matters would be far simpler if you could make the conversion as many times as you liked by simply entering the degrees Fahrenheit and punching a button. Well, knowing how to solve the problem, you know what the automatic program is. It consists of the same steps. All you have to do is key them in.

With the power switch turned ON, set the PRGM−RUN switch to PRGM. As a matter of routine, press f PRGM to clear the calculator of any program already stored. The display reads 00, showing that you are at step 00 and ready to key in your program. Press ENTER 32 − 5 ENTER 9 ÷ × . Your program is stored in registers 00−09 of the calculator's program memory.

Switch from PRGM to RUN and press f PRGM. This time, pressing f PRGM sets the calculator to program step 00. The program is now ready to run—all set to convert any number of degrees F to degrees C. Try it out. Press 98.6 R/S and watch the display. For a brief moment the display will become scrambled, signifying that the program is running; then it will read out 37.00. Now enter 80 (it is not necessary this time to press f PRGM; the calculator has automatically returned to step 00) and press R/S. The answer 26.67 comes up. Key in 212 R/S. The answer is 100. You should be convinced, but press 32 R/S anyway. Does the program also work on below-zero F temperatures? Press 25 CHS R/S and see.

You are now a programmer.

What you have done, of course, is to order the calculator to press the right buttons for you once you have made your *data entry* (in this case the degrees F) and pressed the run/stop key.

Program Checking and Debugging: The Keycodes

As you well may suspect, programming for complex calculations does not always result in first-time success; the chances are that your first do-it-yourself program will exhibit some bugs. Don't feel crushed if that happens; the experts are not immune either. Possibly your program is faulty, but your first effort to unearth the problem should be to make sure that you have entered the program correctly. The HP-25 will, if you ask it to, help you to verify the keyed-in steps one by one according to their keycodes. In addition it will display the calculated results after each step. Let's verify the program you have just entered, even though we know there is nothing wrong with it.

If you have not switched the power OFF, the program is still in the calculator. (Turning off the power clears any program, the four stack registers and the eight memories.) If you have killed the program, set the switches to ON and PRGM, reenter the program and switch to RUN, then press f PRGM to set the calculator to step 00. Enter any temperature, say 75. Now press SST, the single-step key, and hold it down.

The display shows 01 31. These numbers indicate that for step 01 you pressed key 31 (row 3, key 1). Now release the SST key. The display shows 75.00, the number you put in as your data entry. Press SST again and hold it down. The display 02 03 means that in step 02 the 3 key was pressed. Release SST and 3 appears in the display. Carrying the procedure through the nine program steps gives you this set of readouts:

Press SST	01	31	
Release	75.00		
Press SST	02	03	
Release	3.		
Press SST	03	02	
Release	32.		
Press SST	04	41	
Release	43.00		(75 − 32)
Press SST	05	05	
Release	5.		
Press SST	06	31	
Release	5.00		
Press SST	07	09	

(cond. from previous page)

Release	9.			
Press SST	08	71		
Release	0.56		(5 ÷ 9)	(actually 0.555555556)
Press SST	09	61		
Release	23.89		(answer: 43 × 5/9 = 23.88888889 if you press f FIX 9)	

In writing, editing, testing and debugging programs, as well as in analyzing the many prepared programs you will find in the HP-25 Application Programs book, you will find this one-step-at-a-time review process invaluable. Not only does it show you whether you have entered the program as you intended; it will also show you, for a program routine where you have already worked out a sample with the right intermediate and final answers, the stage at which your program became faulty.

Data Entries and Program Initialization

So much for the keying-in and checking-out of the °F/°C program. Our next concern is with getting a program ready to run. Generally, some data entries have to be made and some initialization has to go in. The line between data entry and initialization is not clearly drawn, perhaps, but both are a part of implementing a program. In the temperature-conversion program we have just looked at, some data are included in the program: the values −32 and 5/9; but many routines involve outside-the-program entries. Most data entries consist of numbers that are stored in one of the eight memories, to be recalled and used during the calculation, but it is also possible to store such numbers in the stack. Such steps as pressing f PRGM to set the calculator to program step 00 and fixing the decimal display to other than two places would properly be called parts of program initialization.

In the case at hand there is only one data entry to make, the F temperature. As you will discover presently, other programs, including the rally navigation and scoring programs, require several such entries.

Entering Negative Values

If you wished to convert a below-zero Fahrenheit temperature to Centigrade, say −22°F, you would have to press f PRGM (unless the calculator was already at step 00) and then 22 CHS. Not −22 or 22−, but 22 CHS (change sign). The reason you do not use the minus key is that pressing − always executes the subtraction of the value in R_x from that in R_y. Here you do not want to subtract anything from anything; you only want to render 22 negative. Pressing CHS after the number has been entered accomplishes this. (It also, of course, changes a negative value to a positive one.) If you key in 22 CHS and press R/S the display will give you the Centigrade equivalent, −30.00°.

Iterative Programs

If you suspect that you can develop this basic program to handle a whole series of temperature conversions automatically, you are right, provided the series is rational. Suppose you wish to find the °C equivalents of all the °F from −25 to +75 at 5-degree intervals: −25, −20 . . . +70, +75. You can easily enough program the calculator to solve the equation in this fashion repeatedly by instructing it to add 5° to the previous F temperature after each answer has been reached.

To arrange this repetitive process you will have to elaborate on your basic nine-step program. Since program writing is usually made easier if the requirements are first set down in ordinary language, let's list the desired operations. To begin with we must enter the first F temperature, −25, and store it for subsequent retrieval so that we can later add 5 to it. Then we must tell the calculator that after it has converted −25 it is to find the next temperature, −20.

So we place −25 (25 CHS, remember) in the first memory, R_0. Having already written and tested the conversion program, we can use it pretty much as it stands. But after the conversion of −25°F has been made, we have to start the calculator on a second round, this time to convert −20. In other words, we must command an *unconditional branch*.

Unconditional Branching

An unconditional branch (or loop) is a routine wherein the calculator is ordered to go to some earlier or later program step and proceed from there. (A conditional branch, about which more later, accomplishes the same thing, but only if a conditional test shows the condition to be true or untrue.) What we want now is an unconditional branch that will always add 5 to the number of degrees last converted and cause the calculator to make the new conversion and another and another.

Combining the required elements into a workable program is not difficult if the right commands are given in the right sequence. Sometimes, be warned, what looks like the right way turns up flawed, in which case one must try again. But for our present purpose this would seem to be a logical approach:

00		
01	2	
02	5	
03	CHS	Places -25 in R_x
04	STO 0	Stores -25 in R_0
05	RCL 0	Writes -25 from R_0 to R_x; although this step may appear redundant to step 04, it is not really, as will become clear later
06	3	
07	2	
08	−	Subtracts 32 from -25, writing -57 in R_x
09	5	
10	ENTER	
11	9	
12	÷	Divides 5 by 9
13	×	Multiplies -57 by 5/9; this is the answer to the first conversion
14	f Pause	Displays the answer, -31.67, for about one second
15	5	
16	STO + 0	Increments the value in R_0 by 5; the number in R_0 is now -70
17	GTO 05	Sends the calculator back to step 05, where it recalls the new value in R_0 and begins to calculate the C equivalent of $-70°F$; now you see why steps 04 and 04 2343 needed

To test this program, enter it in PRGM mode, switch to RUN, press f PRGM and R/S. The results are self-evident, the answers coming up every two seconds or so. The program will run indefinitely until the numbers exceed the capacity of the calculator (that will take a good while!) or until you stop program execution by pressing a key. (Pressing any key will do, but the logical one is R/S.)

After having let the program run through a few cycles, you may have lost track of the F temperatures whose C equivalents are being displayed. A minor program modification will fix that. It is not necessary to rewrite the whole program. Still in RUN mode, press GTO 13. Now switch to PRGM mode and key in these new program steps:

14 RCL 0
15 f PAUSE
16 R↓
17 f PAUSE
18 5
19 STO + 0
20 GTO 05

Switch back to RUN and press f PRGM R/S. Now you will see the F temperature displayed just before its corresponding C temperature appears. We have contrived this nicety by recalling the current F value from R_0 (at step 14) and ordering it displayed (step 15). In the meantime step 14 sent the answer, the C value that was calculated in step 13, up the stack into R_y. To bring the answer back we call on R↓(step 16) to roll down the stack and restore the answer to R_x so that it can be displayed in step 17. Steps 18 and 19 add 5 to the temperature value stored in R_0. Step 20 sends the calculator back to step 05, where − 20 is recalled from R_0 ar.d the new calculation is begun.

We have improved the program, surely, but we have not yet perfected it. Remember, we said in the beginning that we wanted to carry the conversions only as far as 75°F. As things stand now, the calculator will keep right on going, to 80°, 85°, 90° and a lot farther. Is it possible to make the calculator stop as soon as it has converted 75°? Well, as Al Jolson was wont to say, you ain't heard nothin' yet.

Conditional Branching

You have just seen how an unconditional branch works: GTO 05, the last step in the program, sends the calculator back to step 05 no matter what; the calculator picks up from there, runs another conversion, returns to step 05, and so indefinitely. Our aim is to make the branch conditional. We want to tell the calculator; "As long as the F temperature value is less than 75, keep on converting; but when you have finished the conversion of 75°, stop."

At this juncture a good look at the $-$, $+$, $\times$ and $\div$ keys is in order. Printed in gold above these keys are these symbols:

$x < y$ (if x is less than y)
$x \geq y$ (if x is equal to or greater than y)
$x \neq y$ (if x is unequal to y)
$x = y$ (if x equals y)

Printed in blue on the slanted faces of the keys are these symbols:

$x < 0$ (if x is less than zero)
$x \geq 0$ (if x is equal to or greater than zero)
$x \neq 0$ (if x is unequal to zero)
$x = 0$ (if x equals zero)

Remarkably, these eight tests comprise all the comparisons that can be made between the magnitudes of any two numbers, or between the the magnitude of any number and zero. They enable the programmer to cause the calculator to test the value in R_x against either the value in R_y or zero. This he does by including the appropriate test instruction in the form of f or g followed by one of the four test keys. At this stage of the program execution the calculator responds in one of two ways. If the answer to the condition is yes, the calculator automatically goes to the next program step; if the answer is no, it automatically skips a step. Represented diagramatically, the process is this:

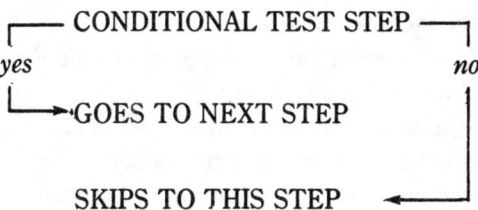

This program feature that sends the calculator in one direction or another, so to speak, depending on the result of a conditional test is called conditional branching. As you can imagine, it puts considerable power in the hands of the HP-25 programmer. He can write one or more such discretionary forks or loops into a program, and in every case the calculator will do what should be done whichever way the test is answered.

As it happens, since we want to compare x with 75 we will use one of the gold-function tests to see how the latest incremented F temperature value in R_x relates to 75 in R_y. Be warned, however, that the choice of tests is not always easy; trying to make the right choice can quickly frazzle your sense of logic. To say no, x is not unequal to y is not always the same as saying yes, x is equal to y; and to say yes, x is less than y is not always the same as saying no, x is not equal to or greater than y. In the case at hand, for instance, you might want to change the temperature increment from 5 to some even number like 2 or 4; if you kept -25 as the starting temperature, an even-numbered increment would never bring the temperature just converted *to* 75. Moreover, if you posited your test, even retaining the 5-degree increment, on x's becoming equal to y, the test $fx = y$ would halt the calculator's operation *before* the 75-degree conversion was made. The best possibility, then, seems to be $fx < y$. As long as x (75) is more than y (the latest incremented temperature), the answer is no, x is not less than y, and we will arrange for the calculator to go through the routine again. When finally x is exceeded by y, the answer will be yes, x is less than y, and we will tell the calculator to make no more conversions and to return to program step 00, stopping the program.

Having established our choice of conditional test, we must now decide where and how to work it into the program. The logical place to insert the conditional branch would seem to be after program step 19, where the incremented-by-5 value of °F has just been written into R_0. We want to write this value momentarily in R_x, then place the limit, 75, in R_x, sending the value in R_x up to R_y, and finally compare the two by asking the calculator whether x is less than y—that is, whether 75 has been exceeded by the most recently incremented F value. If the answer is yes, we will order the calculator to stop (GTO 00 will accomplish this). If the answer is no, we will order the calculator to branch back to the step where it can resume program execution and make another conversion; that, of course, is step 05.

We can leave steps 00–19 as they are and make this further program modification by inserting six new steps beginning with step 20. With the calculator still in RUN mode, press GTO 19, then switch to PRGM and enter these steps:

20	RCL 0	Recalls °F number from R_0 to R_x
21	7	
22	5	Places 75 in R_x, moving the temperature value to R_y
23	$f\ x < y$	Asks whether 75 is less than the F value
24	GTO 00	If the answer is yes, the program goes automatically to this next step, which sends the calculator back to step 00, stopping the program
25	GTO 05	If the answer is no, the program automatically skips step 24 and goes to this step, which sends the calculator back to step 05, where it will execute the rest of the program

Now if you switch to RUN and press f PRGM R/S, the calculator will make all the conversions from -25 to $+75$ and stop.

We have improved the program considerably. Can we make it even more useful? Indeed we can. As it stands now, it is capable only of solving for the twenty-one Centigrade values of Fahrenheit temperatures from -25 to 75 at 5-degree intervals. Suppose we need to convert a different set of values and use a different increment, say 80°F to 110°F at 2-degree intervals. In order to place these new parameters in the calculator we shall have to rewrite several program steps, substituting 80 for 25 CHS in steps 01–03, 110 for 75 in steps 21–22, and 2 for 5 in step 18. These changes will upset the step numbering and force us to rewrite the program completely.

More About Data Entries

A far better way to provide for varying the temperature and increment parameters is to leave them out of the program altogether and load them into the calculator memories as data entries. This significant refinement will produce an all-purpose program, one that will recall the three parameters from memory so that the calculator can operate on them just as it did when they were built into the program. Then when we need to substitute new temperatures and increments we shall be able to load them in the memories without disturbing the program in any way.

We have a choice of eight memory locations for the three numbers. In the interest of orderliness we will store the lower F temperature in R_0, the higher one in R_1 and the increment in R_2. Using our previous program as a general guide, we quite easily come up with this:

00		11	f PAUSE
01	RCL 0	12	R↓
02	3	13	f PAUSE
03	2	14	RCL 2
04	−	15	STO + 0
05	5	16	RCL 0
06	ENTER	17	RCL 1
07	9	18	f x < y
08	÷	19	GTO 00
09	×	20	GTO 01
10	RCL 0		

Switch the calculator OFF to clear out the old program. Turn the power ON again and set the other switch to PRGM. Enter the program. To load the three parameters, switch to RUN and key them in:

80 STO 0   110 STO 1   2 STO 2

Then: f PRGM R/S . . . *quod erat demonstrandum*.

Now you say you want the C values of F temperatures from −10 to 0 in increments of 2 1/2 degrees? Just enter the new data:

10 CHS STO 0   0 STO 1   2.5 STO 2   f PRGM R/S

To evaluate what we have done here, note first that we have boiled the program down to twenty steps from twenty-five. This lesson in program economy is meaningful because the number of program steps is limited to forty-nine, and there may be times when keeping within that number will test your ingenuity. In any case, the fewer the steps the faster the program runs; and on principle it is deemed *au fait* always to use as few steps as possible. Even more important is that we have rendered this latest program much more adaptable by resorting to preloading data entries as a method of introducing parameter values, which we can now change easily, quickly and as often as we please.

Of course you are wondering about step 12:R↓, a newcomer. It is a time- and step-saver. If you review the program step by step using the SST key in RUN mode you will perceive that step 09 is the final step in the conversion routine. In step 10 we recall from R_0 the F temperature just converted so that we can display it in step 11. Step 09 sends the just-calculated C value up the stack into R_y, where we leave it parked, so to speak, while we display the F number in step 11. Step 12 rolls down the stack, returning the C answer to R_x, whence it is displayed in step 13.

As remarked at the beginning of this chapter, temperature conversions have absolutely nothing to do with rallying. But the programs we have constructed demonstrate a number of principles that apply in the rally navigation and rally scoring programs that are developed in the chapters to follow: adapting a series of manual keystrokes to automatic program steps; entering, storing and retrieving data; recalling intermediate and final answers from memory and from the stack; ordering unconditional branches and, with the aid of the eight logic-test keys, conditional branches—to mention just a few. Now we can leave the object-lessons and see how the HP-25 will solve the rally average-speed problem.

Chapter 4
HP-25 Rally Navigation

IF YOU ARE new at calculator programming, and if the preceding chapter has boggled your brain a bit (as it well may have if you don't yet have an HP-25 to work with), take heart. The programs for rally navigation are quite straightforward and uncomplicated and without branches—although you will see a number of conditional branches later on in the rally scoring programs. Probably you have already noticed the three variations of HP-25 navigation programs printed, for ready reference, in the Appendix of this book. If you are to use them to best advantage you should understand how they work. We'll begin with the basic program and see how it was formulated.

The logical first step in devising any system is to ask not how to do it but what do we want it to do. Ideally, a rally navigation system should:

1. Calculate, as often as desired, the driving time—corrected for odometer error—allowed by the prescribed average speed for any distance.
2. Display that distance in miles to the nearest hundredth.
3. Display the allowed time, properly rounded, in whichever way suits the timepieces in use: as elapsed (stopwatch) time in minutes and seconds or in minutes and hundredths, or as true time of day (clock time).
4. Calculate and display on demand the official distance driven.

5. Calculate and display on demand the odometer-distance equivalent of any official distance.
6. Provide a direct and simple method of negotiating mid-leg changes of average speed.
7. Permit handling "pause" and gain-time" instructions by increasing or decreasing the allowed driving time independently of distance.
8. Permit convenient and effective coping with the arithmetic of time lost off course.
9. Display on demand, for checking or rechecking, any or all stored data or current answers.
10. Accomplish all this without requiring the use of more than one odometer or more than one watch or clock, and without making it necessary to reset or adjust the odometer or the timepiece between scoring checkpoints.

Are these many desiderata too tall an order for a tiny six-ounce calculator? Let's find out by essaying to adapt these requirements to the HP-25's capabilities. The temptation is strong to imitate the Curta system, which is based on a strictly incremental succession of distance inputs. Tried, true and unquestionably serviceable, the Curta method has one acknowledged weakness: the considerable carriage shifting, crank turning and slide manipulation required at speed changes. To duplicate the Curta routine for the HP-25 is, as a matter of fact, easy enough; however, such a program does not ameliorate the concomitant awkwardnesses of changing speeds. There must be a better way . . .

The raw data available to us are these:
1. The stated average speed.
2. The official length of the odometer check.
3. Our odometer reading at the end of the odometer check.
4. The distance driven according to our odometer.

That's all we have to work with—and all we need. Now to take these bits and pieces and put them together rationally, let's start by loading into the calculator memories the parameters with which we must operate. We will store them, quite arbitrarily, this way:

The average speed in R_2.
60 in R_3 (we can anticipate having to divide 60 by the official

average speed to get the uncorrected minutes-per-mile factor).

Factor A (the official distance of the odometer check divided by our indicated distance) in R_4.

Factor B (the indicated distance divided by the official distance) in R_5.

These storage registers we will reserve:

R_0 for the accumulated allowed time.
R_1 for the current odometer distance.
R_6 for the official distance.
R_7 for use in a later, more elaborate program.

Applying ourselves to the arithmetic of the average-speed problem, we can readily see the operations to be performed:

1. Divide 60 by the stated average speed to get the uncorrected minutes-per-mile factor.
2. Multiply the uncorrected minutes-per-mile factor by Factor A to get the corrected minutes-per-mile factor.
3. Multiply the driven distance by the corrected minutes-per-mile factor to find the corrected allowed time for driving that distance.
4. Display momentarily, as a visual check, the driven distance; and then display the corrected allowed time either in minutes and seconds or in minutes and hundredths (we'll get to time-of-day time presently).
5. Calculate and store in R_6 the official distance equivalent to the odometer distance accumulated in R_1.

This series of operations is obviously elementary and easily arranged. But if we are to avoid the Curta's rather awkward expedient of building up indicated distance from successively added mileage constants, we encounter a problem when we try to produce displays of mileage and corresponding allowed times that will survive a speed change. To explain:

Suppose that our corrected minutes-per-mile factor is 2.123. Keying in 1 and multiplying gives 2.123 minutes for 1 mile; multiplying by 2 gives 4.246 minutes for 2 miles. But if at 2 miles we have to change to a new speed for which the minutes-per-mile factor happens to be 1.987, we cannot now multiply 1.987 by 3 and get the allowed time at the end of 3 miles.

It dawns on us, painfully, that we are going to have to settle for some kind of incremental system after all. So be it. But why not let the *calculator* calculate the increment?

It would seem that we ought to be able to accomplish this objective in three stages by causing the calculator first to subtract the last previously entered distance from the newly entered distance, then to calculate the allowed time for the difference (which is in effect an increment) and finally to add that time to the stored time allowed for the previous distance. The method having been stated, it is no trouble at all to work up a program that will allow us always to deal directly with the distance driven *as shown by the odometer*.

HP-25 AVERAGE-SPEED NAVIGATION PROGRAM I

Calculates allowed time as elapsed (stopwatch) time in minutes and hundredths of minutes

00		09	×
01	RCL 1	10	STO + 0
02	–	11	RCL 1
03	STO + 1	12	RCL 4
04	RCL 3	13	×
05	RCL 2	14	STO 6
06	÷	15	RCL 1
07	RCL 4	16	*f* PAUSE
08	×	17	RCL 0

(To display the allowed times in minutes and seconds add step 18: *f* H.MS.)

Before making data entries, switch to RUN.
Data Entries
1. Average speed in miles per hour STO 2
2. 60 STO 3
3. Factor A:
   official distance of odometer check
   ENTER
   car odometer reading at end of odometer check
   ÷ STO 4

4. Factor B:
    with Factor A still in R$_x$:
    g 1/x STO 5

Program Initialization
1. f PRGM
2. Key in distance in miles (or miles and hundredths) for which the allowed time is wanted
3. R/S
4. For subsequent time checks key in the distance and press R/S

Callouts

Between program runs—

RCL 0 displays accumulated allowed time
RCL 1 displays last entered odometer distance
RCL 2 displays the average speed in use
RCL 3 displays 60
RCL 4 displays Factor A
RCL 5 displays Factor B
RCL 6 displays the official-distance equivalent of the distance stored in R$_1$

To Change Average Speed
1. Key in the odometer reading at the speed-change point
2. R/S
3. Key in the new average speed
4. STO 2
5. Key in the next odometer distance for which the allowed time is wanted
6. R/S

For the Odometer Equivalent of an Official Distance
1. Key in the official distance
2. RCL 5 ×

Pause (Lose Time)

Key in amount of time to be lost:
  a. as minutes and hundredths GTO 10 R/S
  b. as minutes and seconds g H GTO 10 R/S

Gain Time

Key in the amount of time to be gained:
a. as minutes and hundredths CHS GTO 10 R/S
b. as minutes and hundredths g H CHS GTO 10 R/S

Procedure at End of Leg

1. 0 STO 0 STO 1 (clears R_0 and R_1; it is unnecessary to clear R_6)
2. If there is a new average speed, store it in R_2
3. Key in first odometer distance for which the allowed time is wanted and press R/S

Time Displays After One Hour

Note that allowed times of one hour or more will be displayed in minutes: 1 hr. 3.6 min. will be shown as 63.60; if program step 18 is in use it will be shown as 63.36 (63 min. 36 sec.)

How the Program Works

Step 01 recalls the previous odometer distance (at the start of a leg this will of course be 0.00).

Step 02 subtracts this distance from the distance just entered; the difference is the distance driven since the previous check.

Step 03 adds this difference to the previous distance stored in R_1; R_1 now contains the current distance.

Step 04 recalls 60 from R_3.

Step 05 recalls the average speed from R_2.

Step 06 divides 60 by the average speed, giving the uncorrected minutes-per-mile factor.

Step 07 recalls Factor A from R_4.

Step 08 multiplies the uncorrected minutes-per-mile factor by Factor A, giving the corrected minutes-per-mile factor.

Step 09 multiplies the distance difference (obtained in Step 02) by the corrected minutes-per-mile factor, giving the corrected allowed time for the distance increment.

Step 10 adds this allowed time to the allowed time accumulated in R_0.

Step 11 recalls the current total odometer distance from R_1.

Step 12 recalls Factor A.

Step 13 multiplies the current total odometer distance by Factor A, giving the total official distance.

Step 14 writes the current total official distance in R_6.

Step 15 again recalls the current total odometer distance from R_1.

Step 16 displays the current total odometer distance for about one second.

Step 17 recalls and displays the total allowed driving time for the current total odometer distance in minutes and hundredths.

Step 18 displays the allowed time in minutes and seconds.

A comprehensive run-through in the form of a typical rally will be made in the next chapter. But to take a quick look at how Program I shapes up, load it into the calculator (omitting step 18 for the moment) and then enter these data:

average speed 30 mph	30 STO 2
constant 60	60 STO 3
Factor A: assume an odometer check of 10.00 official miles and an odometer reading of 9.97 miles	10 ENTER 9.97 ÷ STO 4
Factor B: with Factor A still in R_x	g 1/x STO 5

Press successively: f PRGM, then—

1 R/S	display: 1.00 (mile)	2.01 (min.)
2 R/S	display: 2.00 (miles)	4.01 (min.)
3 R/S	display: 3.00 (miles)	6.02 (min.)

Now suppose that a speed change to 40 mph comes up at 3.45 miles. Press:

3.45 R/S	display: 3.45 (miles)	6.92 (min.)
40 STO 2		
4 R/S	display: 4.00 (miles)	7.75 (min.)
5 R/S	display: 5.00 (miles)	9.25 (min.)

Could anything be simpler?

Now try the same routine with step 18 added. Still in RUN mode, press GTO 17; switch to PRGM; key in f H.MS; switch back to RUN; press 0 STO 0 STO 1 f PRGM (to clear R_0 and R_1 and to send the calculator to step 00); 30 STO 2.

Press in succession again:

1 R/S	display: 1.00 (mile)		2.00 (2 min. 0 sec.)
2 R/S	display: 2.00 (miles)		4.00 (4 min. 0 sec.)
3 R/S	display: 3.00 (miles)		6.01 (6 min. 1 sec.)
3.45 R/S	display: 3.45 (miles)		6.55 (6 min. 55 sec.)
40 STO 2			
4 R/S	display: 4.00 (miles)		7.45 (7 min. 45 sec.)
5 R/S	display: 5.00 (miles)		9.15 (9 min. 15 sec.)

That is all very well, you say, except that last month you hurled your stopwatch at the chairman of the protest committee and now have to navigate with a chronograph that tells only time of day. All right, here's your program:

HP-25 AVERAGE-SPEED NAVIGATION PROGRAM II

Calculates allowed time as clock time (time of day) in hours, minutes and seconds

00			12	RCL 3
01	*f* FIX 2		13	÷
02	RCL 1		14	STO + 7
03	−		15	RCL 1
04	STO + 1		16	RCL 4
05	RCL 3		17	×
06	RCL 2		18	STO 6
07	÷		19	RCL 1
08	RCL 4		20	*f* PAUSE
09	×		21	RCL 7
10	×		22	*f* FIX 4
11	STO + 0		23	*f* H.MS

The data entries for Program II are exactly the same as those for Program I with a single addition: you must store your starting time in R_7. This time must be keyed in as hours, decimal point, minutes and seconds, as HP-25 notation requires, *followed by g H STO 7*. If your starting time is 9:07:00 (exactly 7 minutes past 9 o'clock) you key in 9.07 *g* H STO 7. If it is 9:07:19 (7 minutes 19 seconds past 9) you key in 9.0719 *g* H STO 7.

Program II resembles Program I with only a few exceptions. Step 10 calculates the corrected allowed time, in minutes and hundredths, for the latest distance increment. Step 11 adds this time to the time stored in R_0. At this point the time is still displayed as the contents of R_x. Steps 12 and 13 divide the time by 60, converting the decimal minutes to decimal hours. Step 14 adds the decimal-hours time to the accumulated time in R_7. Step 21 recalls the total decimal-hour time-of-day time. Step 22 fixes four decimal places. Step 23 changes the decimal-hour time to hours, minutes and seconds and displays it as clock time.

Check Program II using the same data entries plus 9.07 g H STO 7. Now:

1 R/S	display: 1.00 (mile)	9.0900 (9:09:00)
2 R/S	display: 2.00 (miles)	9.1101 (9:11:01)
3 R/S	display: 3.00 (miles)	9.1301 (9:13:01)
3.45 R/S	display: 3.45 (miles)	9.1355 (9:13:55)
40 STO 2		
4 R/S	display: 4.00 (miles)	9.1445 (9:14:45)
5 R/S	display: 5.00 (miles)	9.1615 (9:16:15)

If you compare the displays here with those obtained from Program I using step 18, you will detect a discrepancy in the allowed times for 2 miles. Program II gives 4 minutes 1 second; Program I gave 4 minutes 0 seconds. The reason is that Program I times are converted at step 18 from minutes and hundredths to minutes and seconds, while in Program II the computational base is decimal hours. The discrepancy evolves where the expression is rounded off, and it is unavoidable, given the nature of the calculator, which when dealing with hours, minutes and seconds is accurate only (!) to five decimal places. You will be encouraged to observe, however, that beginning with the 3-mile reading the allowed time reestablishes—and maintains—accuracy to the second.

On this same subject, be warned that in the hours-minutes-seconds mode the calculator may occasionally startle you with a readout like this: 11.2360—11 hours 23 minutes 60 seconds. Don't let your faith be shaken; the calculator is not malfunctioning. On the contrary, it is doing precisely what it was designed to do. It has rounded, for the display, 59+ seconds to 60; however, since it knows quite well that 59+ is less than 60, it has not turned over to the next minute. For this kind of precision you must agree that having once in a while to mentally change such a figure as 23 minutes 60 seconds to 24 minutes is a small price to pay.

Program II is all right too, you say, but your hundredths-of-minutes-reading stopwatch just came back from having been repaired and you've decided you'd like to use it and your time-of-day chronograph both. The best of both temporal worlds is contained in Program III, which presents the allowed time for any distance as decimal-minute elapsed time *and* as hours-minutes-seconds true time of day.

HP-25 AVERAGE-SPEED NAVIGATION PROGRAM III

Calculates allowed time as elapsed (stopwatch) time in minutes and hundredths of minutes and as clock time (time of day) in hours, minutes and seconds

00		13	÷
01	*f* FIX 2	14	STO + 7
02	RCL 1	15	RCL 1
03	−	16	RCL 4
04	STO + 1	17	×
05	RCL 3	18	STO 6
06	RCL 2	19	RCL 1
07	÷	20	*f* PAUSE
08	RCL 4	21	RCL 0
09	×	22	*f* PAUSE
10	×	23	RCL 7
11	STO + 0	24	*f* FIX 4
12	RCL 3	25	*f* H.MS

The data entries for Program III are the same as those for Program II; indeed, Program III is only a slight modification of Program II.

As you will readily surmise, where a rally leg commences in the morning and lasts past noon, the time-of-day displays in these two programs will automatically read in military— 24-hour—time when the accumulated allowed clock time goes beyond 12.5959. If you wish, you can subtract 12 hours and restore the display to conventional clock time. Pressing 12 STO − 7 turns 13 o'clock to 1 o'clock.

The Odometer Check

During the odometer calibration run no attempt is made to adhere to an average speed even though one may be stated. If the instructions read, "The odometer check is 10.00 official miles and the average speed is 30 mph," you know that you can—and should—cover the ground in less than 20 minutes and have time enough in hand to calculate your odometer error and do whatever else is necessary before starting the next part of the rally. Nevertheless, a good way to handle the calculations associated with the odometer check is to treat it as though it were an average-speed section.

When you arrive at the marker ending the run, note your odometer reading, move on, park and get out your calculator. If you have not entered your program en route, do so now. Make your data entries:

30 STO 2
60 STO 3
Assuming that your odometer read 9.95 at the end of the check:
10 ENTER 9.95 ÷ STO 4
g 1/x STO 5
If you are using Program II or III, store your starting time in R_7—not forgetting to follow it with g H STO 7.
And finally:
f PRGM 9.95 R/S

This first run of the program is as good a way as any of producing the displays you need:

9.95 (miles) and 20.00 (minutes).

If the average speed changes at the end of the odometer check, store it now in R_2. If not, leave R_2 as it is. In either case your next calculator operation will be to press 10 R/S; then 11 R/S, and so on.

What if no average speed for the odometer check is stated? Then you can calculate it. Suppose the check is 20.00 official miles with 35 minutes allowed. Remember:

$$\text{speed in mph} = \frac{\text{miles} \times 60}{\text{minutes}}$$

So key in 20 ENTER 60 × 35 ÷ STO 2, which puts 34.29 (mph) in R_2.

No Odometer Error

Once in a great while, by the merest happenstance, you may come to the end of an odometer check and find that your odometer reading is identical to the announced official distance. This state of affairs, happily regarded by many rallyists as a good omen (though it makes not the slightest difference to the HP-25), is commonly called "zero odometer error." And so it is. The calculator, however, will not take kindly to 0 for Factors A and B in R_4 and R_5. On the contrary, it will retaliate to your asking it to multiply (or divide) a number by zero by giving you wrong answers or displaying "Error."

Factors A and B, you should recognize, are *ratios*, and a ratio is always a real number. If at the end of 10.00 official miles your odometer reads 10.00, dividing the former by the latter gives 1, and you must key in 1 STO 4 STO 5.

Other Distance Units

What would you do if you found yourself in a *metric* rally where all distances were given in kilometers and all speeds in kilometers per hour, while your odometer and speedometer read only in miles and miles per hour? Rummage around for a conversion table? No need. It is quite unnecessary to know how many kilometers there are in a mile, or vice versa. Just carry on as you would in a conventional rally and let your odometer difference take care of everything automatically.

Suppose you had these instructions:

> The odometer check is 35.00 km. long, and the average speed is 65.00 km./hr. At 56.78 km. turn right.

First you need the time allowed for the odometer check. You know it is (35 × 60) ÷ 65; 35 ENTER 60 × 65 ÷ gives it: 32.31 minutes.

At the end of the odometer check your odometer reads 21.75 miles. Calculate Factor A in the usual way: 35 ÷ 21.75 = 1.61; Factor B, then, is 0.62. That these factors are of unusual magnitude makes no difference to the calculator, and you should not let it make any difference to you.

Using any of the navigation programs, you will find that the time allowed for one odometer mile is 1.49 min., or 1 min. 29 sec. What speed is that in terms of your odometer? RCL2 RCL5 × multiplies the stated speed by Factor B and tells you: 40.39 mph. Where will you find the right turn? RCL 5 56.78 × gives you the odometer distance: 35.28 miles.

Once you have hurdled the mental block thrown up by the abnormally large odometer difference, you will find that the programs function exactly as usual. This would be true if the official distances were measured in nautical miles and the speeds stated in knots.

Time-based Route Directions

A "time-based" rally instruction is one that requires you to take some action at a particular moment. For example: "The average speed is 30 mph. Exactly 20 1/2 minutes after starting this leg, turn right." If you happen to be exactly on time at the critical juncture, you have nothing to worry about. If not, you had better know what your odometer reading should be at that point. Assuming no odometer error, no changes in average speed, no pauses and no gains, after 20 1/2 minutes your odometer should read 10.25 miles. You may rest assured, however, that within that brief time span you will be dealing with a generous assortment of speed changes, pauses and gains, each of which will alter the projected time-defined distance. You need, obviously, a method of successively reestimating that distance until the most recent estimate becomes the definitive one.

Navigational Program I can readily be supplemented to handle this complication. You merely tack on a dozen program steps and store the given time (as minutes and hundredths) in R_7. Running this portion of the program at each speed change and at each pause or gain will update and display the required distance figure. When you have handled the last speed change, pause, gain or whatever, the latest calculated time-based distance is the right one. This is how the modified program looks:

Keycodes			*Keystrokes*	*Keycodes*			*Keystrokes*
00				08		61	×
01		24 01	RCL 1	09		61	×
02		41	−	10	23 51	00	STO + 0
03	23 51	01	STO + 1	11		24 01	RCL 1
04		24 03	RCL 3	12		24 04	RCL 4
05		24 02	RCL 2	13		61	×
06		71	÷	14	23 06		STO 6
07		24 04	RCL 4	15		24 01	RCL 1

(cont. from previous page)

Keycodes		Keystrokes	Keycodes		Keystrokes
16	14 74	f PAUSE	24	61	×
17	24 00	RCL 0	25	24 03	RCL 3
18*	15 74	g NOP	26	71	÷
19	13 00	GTO 00	27	24 05	RCL 5
20	24 07	RCL 7	28	61	×
21	24 00	RCL 0	29	24 01	RCL 1
22	41	–	30	51	+
23	24 02	RCL 2			

Let's check this routine assuming that your odometer read 10.05 at 10.00 official miles. Initialize thus:

0 STO 0 STO 1   10 ENTER 10.05 ÷ STO 4
30 STO 2   g 1/x STO 5
60 STO 3   20.5 STO 7
              f PRGM

Pressing 1 R/S gives you the allowed time for the first mile: 1.99 minutes. Then if you press GTO 20 R/S the first calculation of the distance for 20.5 minutes is made and displayed: 10.30 odometer miles. To get the time allowed for 2 miles, press 2 R/S; the answer is 3.98 minutes. Now, just to satisfy yourself that everything is working right, press GTO 20 R/S again. Again the distance for 20.5 minutes is displayed as 10.30 miles. This of course is as it should be; until a speed change, a pause or a gain takes place, the projected odometer reading for 20.5 minutes will remain 10.30 miles.

How does this supplementary routine work? Steps 20–22 subtract the elapsed time in R_0 from the given time, initially 20.5 minutes, stored in R_7; the remainder is the amount of time left to go. Steps 23–26 convert the remainder to official miles at the current average speed. Steps 27–28 multiply official miles by Factor B to give odometer miles. Steps 29–30 add to that distance the distance already driven according to the contents of R_1. The sum displayed is the currently calculated time-determined distance. Plainly, it is sub-

---

*If you want the allowed running times displayed as minutes and seconds rather than as minutes and hundredths, key in step 18 as f H.MS.

ject to revision. Any change to a higher average speed, and any gaining of time, will increase the distance; lower average speeds and pauses will shorten it.

Suppose that, as you drive this leg, these things take place:
1. At 3.45 miles the average speed changes to 33 mph
2. At 5.67 miles there is a 2-minute pause
3. At 8.97 miles the average speed changes to 36 mph

Here are the keystrokes and the readouts for the section:

Keystrokes	Readouts	
	miles	minutes
1 R/S	1.00	1.99
GTO 20 R/S	10.30 (miles)	
2 R/S	2.00	3.98
3 R/S	3.00	5.97
3.45 R/S	3.45	6.87
33 STO 2		
GTO 20 R/S	10.99 (miles)	
4 R/S	4.00	7.86
5 R/S	5.00	9.67
5.67 R/S	5.67	10.88
2 GTO 10 R/S	5.67	12.88
GTO 20 R/S	9.88 (miles)	
6 R/S	6.00	13.48
7 R/S	7.00	15.29
8 R/S	8.00	17.10
8.97 R/S	8.97	18.85
36 STO 2		
GTO 20 R/S	9.96 (miles)	
9 R/S	9.00	19.80
And finally, to verify:		
9.96 R/S	9.96	20.49

The last calculation contains a discrepancy of 1/100 minute. This is a rounding error and is immaterial. Turn right at 9.96 miles by your odometer, then look to be on time at the next whole mile:

| 10 R/S | 10.00 | 20.56 |

Note that this supplementary routine for time-based directions can be used only in conjunction with navigation Program I. Programs

II and III, which display allowed driving time and clock time, use all eight of the calculator memories. If in previewing route instructions you discover time-based directions, use Program I for that part of the rally.

Simultaneous Displays

Some navigators, perhaps especially those accustomed to rallying with Curta calculators, like the idea of having distance and time shown simultaneously. The HP-25 can, in many cases, be made to display two sets of figures at once, provided you are willing to furnish mentally the extra decimal point. The trick is to multiply one number by a sufficiently large power of 10 to move it well to the left, and then to add the other number to it. Only one decimal point can be displayed, and it automatically associates itself with the number at the right-hand end of the display. Here is navigation Program I modified to show the odometer distance at the left and the corresponding allowed time at the right:

HP-25 Navigation Program I Modified for Simultaneous Display of Distance and Time.

Keycodes			Keystrokes	Keycodes			Keystrokes
00				11		24 04	RCL 4
01		24 01	RCL 1	12		24 01	RCL 1
02		41	−	13		61	×
03	23 51 01		STO + 1	14		23 06	STO 6
04		24 03	RCL 3	15		24 01	RCL 1
05		24 02	RCL 2	16		33	EEX
06		71	÷	17		05	5
07		24 04	RCL 4	18		61	×
08		61	×	19		24 00	RCL 0
09		61	×	20*		15 74	*g* NOP
10	23 51 00		STO + 0	21		51	+

Steps 01−14 are identical to those of Program I. Step 15 retrieves the odometer reading that was stored in R_1 at step 03; steps 16−18 multiply it by 100,000 (10^5); step 19 places the allowed time in R_x; step 21 adds the allowed time to the distance parked in R_y and displays the combination of numbers.

---

*If you want the time displayed as minutes and seconds, use *f* H.MS for step 20 (keycode 20 14 00).

Try out this program. Key it in, checking the keycodes as you go along. Then initialize, assuming that your odometer read 9.88 at the 10.00-mile check and that the average speed is 33.3 mph:

33.3 STO 2   10 ENTER 9.88 ÷ STO 4
60 STO 3   g 1/x STO 5
                        f PRGM

To show the distance with the allowed time for 1 mile press 1 R/S. The display produces 100001.82, which you must interpret as 1.0000 mile and 1.82 minutes. Then 10 R/S gives 1000018.24—that is, 10.000 miles and 18.24 minutes. Similarly, 100 R/S displays 10000182.37, or 100.00 miles and 182.37 minutes. Fractional distances are keyed in as usual: 12.34 R/S displays 1234022.50 for 12.340 miles and 22.50 minutes.

Program II, which calculates allowed time as time of day, also can be modified for simultaneous display.

HP-25 Navigation Program II Modified for Simultaneous Display of Distance and Time

Keycodes	Keystrokes	Keycodes	Keystrokes
00			
01 14 11 02	f FIX 2	14 23 51 07	STO + 7
02 24 01	RCL 1	15 24 01	RCL 1
03 41	−	16 24 04	RCL 4
04 23 51 01	STO + 1	17 61	×
05 24 03	RCL 3	18 23 06	STO 6
06 24 02	RCL 2	19 24 01	RCL 1
07 71	÷	20 33	EEX
08 24 04	RCL 4	21 04	4
09 61	×	22 61	×
10 61	×	23 24 07	RCL 7
11 23 51 00	STO + 0	24 14 11 04	f FIX 4
12 24 03	RCL 3	25 14 00	f H.MS
13 71	÷	26 51	+

Initialize as before:

33.3 STO 2   10 ENTER 9.88 ÷ STO 4

60 STO 3   g 1/x STO 5

Assuming a leg starting time of 9:07:00 a.m.:

9.07 g→H STO 7   f PRGM

To calculate the time of day at which you should cover, say, 1.00 mile, 9.86 miles and 99.99 miles:

Keystrokes	Display
1 R/S	10009.0849
9.86 R/S	98609.2459
99.99 R/S	999912.0921

Not that you are likely to encounter a rally leg of a hundred miles or more, but you should know that this simultaneous-display program will not work for distances greater than 99.99 miles. Key in 100 R/S and the reason will become evident immediately.

Program III can be similarly treated:

HP-25 Navigation Program III Modified for Simultaneous Display of Distance and Time

Keycodes			Keystrokes	Keycodes			Keystrokes
00							
01	14	11 02	f FIX 2	18		23 06	STO 6
02		24 01	RCL 1	19		24 01	RCL 1
03		41	−	20		33	EEX
04	23	51 01	STO + 1	21		04	4
05		24 03	RCL 3	22		61	×
06		24 02	RCL 2	23		24 00	RCL 0
07		71	÷	24		51	+
08		24 04	RCL 4	25		14 74	f PAUSE
09		61	×	26		14 74	f PAUSE
10		61	×	27		24 01	RCL 1
11	23	51 00	STO + 0	28		33	EEX
12		24 03	RCL 3	29		04	4
13		71	÷	30		61	×
14	23	51 07	STO + 7	31		24 07	RCL 7
15		24 01	RCL 1	32	14	11 04	f FIX 4
16		24 04	RCL 4	33		14 00	f H.MS
17		61	×	34		51	+

You can check this program by entering it and then initializing it just as you did modified Program II. Whether two *consecutive* simultaneous displays are useful is up to you to decide; at any rate they are available if you want them. Again, this program is limited to odometer distances no greater than 99.99 miles.

Chapter 5
Testing the
HP-25 Rally Programs

TO SEE EXACTLY how the programmed HP-25 performs a typical gamut of navigational operations, let's take it on a short but representative simulated rally—a kitchen-table event in which, for once, you will not have to worry about getting lost. Using our most elaborate program, Program III (very possibly the one you will elect to use in actual competition), we shall see what goes into the calculator and, equally interesting if not more so, what comes out.

The equipment we shall theoretically be using is minimal: one nonreversing hundredths-reading odometer; one stopwatch calibrated in minutes and hundredths of minutes; a time-of-day clock or chronograph with a settable second hand; pencils and paper (no matter what system of navigation one uses, it is folly not to make notes of distances and times at every action point); our HP-25; and, needless to say, a copy of this book.

Here are your routeless instructions (the cumulative distances in parentheses are *your* odometer readings):

1. Your car number is 7, and your starting time is 9 a.m. plus your car number in minutes. *(00.00 miles)*
2. The length of the odometer check is 20.00 official miles; you are allowed 37 1/2 minutes for this run. *(20.07 miles)*
3. Proceed from the end of the odometer check at the average speed equivalent to that allowed for the check run.

4. Exactly 5 miles after leaving the end of the odometer check increase your average speed by 10%.
5. Within 2 miles after traffic light *(27.27 miles)* pause for 2 minutes 18 seconds.
6. At T change average speed to 43.2 mph. *(31.99 miles)*
7. At stop sign *(38.78 miles)* change average speed to 24 mph and suppose that a phantom car has left this point 3 minutes before you were due to arrive here. The phantom car's average speed is 20 mph. At the point where you overtake the phantom car, turn right and change your average speed to 34.5 mph.
8. Turn left 45.67 miles from the start of the rally.
9. Within 4 miles after having executed instruction 8 gain 40 seconds.
10. At T reduce average speed by 10% *(54.08 miles)*
11. After passing red barn turn left.

We enter Program III in PRGM mode. Then we check the keycodes to make sure we have it right. (Switch to RUN, press f PRGM, then use the single-step key SST to compare the codes with those printed in the Appendix and press f PRGM once more.) We load our starting time in R_7 by pressing 9.07 g H STO 7. Now we are ready to start rallying, with our imaginary odometer and our imaginary stopwatch zeroed and our imaginary chronometer running to the second on time of day. Off we go through the odometer check.

Reading over the instructions, we see that during the first 20 official miles we shall have to find, for use at instruction 3, the average speed allowed for the odometer check. Pressing 20 ENTER 60 × 37.5 ÷ does it: 32 mph.

Natually, we want to complete the odometer check with time to spare, so we drive as expeditiously as conditions permit. En route we may as well go to work on instruction 7. The formula we need for a phantom car going away, where it has started E minutes before us, is in the Appendix:

$$D = \frac{A \times B \times E}{60\,(B - A)}$$

where A = speed of phantom car in miles per hour
B = speed of rally car in miles per hour

D = miles rally car must travel to catch phantom car
E = minutes phantom car is ahead at start

In this case $A = 20$ (mph)
$B = 24$ (mph)
$E = 3$ (minutes)

Substituting these values in the equation:

$$D = \frac{20 \times 24 \times 3}{60 \,(24 - 20)}$$

In RUN mode—remember, we can use the calculator for side calculations as long as it is not running a program—we derive the answer thus:

20 ENTER 24 × 3 ×
24 ENTER 20 − 60 × ÷

And we find that $D = 6$ official miles. Since we cannot determine our indicated equivalent of 6 miles until we have established our odometer difference, we note the official distance and postpone the conversion.

At the 20.00-mile marker we find that our odometer reads slightly slow: 20.07 miles. It is time to make our data entries, in RUN mode of course:

32 STO 2	Average speed in R_2
60 STO 3	Constant 60 in R_3
20 ENTER 20.07 ÷ STO 4	Factor A in R_4
g 1/x STO 5	Factor B in R_5
f PRGM	Calculator at program step 00

And now:

20.07 R/S displays:	20.07 (miles)
	37.50 (minutes)
	9.4430 (9:44:30 clock time)

When we leave the odometer check, the first thing we shall want to know is the allowed time for 21 indicated miles.

21 R/S displays:	21.00 (miles)
	39.24 (minutes)
	9.4614 (9:46:14 clock time)

If we decide that we want to check every half mile, we may feel free to do so:

21.5 R/S displays·   21.50 (miles)
                          40.17 (minutes)
                          9.4710 (9:47:10 clock time)

There, as simple and direct as we could wish, is our time-checking routine. In goes the distance; out comes the time.

Anticipating instruction 4, we perform a side calculation between program runs in order to find out what our odometer will read at 25.00 official miles from the start of the rally:

25 RCL 5 ×   Multiples 25 by Factor B and gives the answer: 25.09

We make a note of that. Now is as good a time as any to find our odometer equivalent of 6 official miles for instruction 7.

6 RCL 5 ×   Multiples 6 by Factor B and gives the answer: 6.02

We make a note of that too. We also need to know the new average speed called for by instruction 4:

32 ENTER 10 $g\%$ + *or*

RCL 2 10 $g\%$ + Adds 10 percent of 32 to 32 and gives the answer: 35.2 (mph)

We make another note.
At 25.09 miles we change speed:

25.09 R/S displays: 25.09 (miles)
                          46.88 (minutes)
                          9.5353 (clock time)
35.2 STO 2   Stores new speed in R_2
26 R/S displays: 26.00 (miles)
                          48.43 (minutes)
                          9.5526 (clock time)

Now you can appreciate the rewards that come from having eliminated the Curta type of incremental distance inputs!

The traffic light in instruction 5 comes up at 27.27 miles.

27.27 R/S displays: 27.27 (miles)
                          50.58 (minutes)
                          9.5735 (clock time)

Here we have to add 2 minutes 18 seconds to our allowed time. Remember, it is imperative to change minutes and seconds to decimal minutes. So:

2.18 g H   Converts 2:18 to 2.30 minutes
*GTO 11 R/S displays: 27.27 (miles)
                            52.88 (minutes)
                            9.5953 (clock time)

As you see, the distance reading is the same—27.27 miles—but 2.3 minutes have been added to the stopwatch time and 2 minutes 18 seconds have been added to the clock time. We have accomplished this by sending the calculator through a partial program run. At step 11, 2.3 is added to the allowed time stored in R_0; steps 12–13 convert 2.3 minutes to decimal hours (0.038333333 hour, although you don't see it done); and step 14 adds this time to the clock time stored in R_7. Steps 15–18 merely recalculate the official distance already stored in R_6. Steps 19–25 produce the new set of displays.

Now we have a free zone of 2.00 official miles—very nearly the same as 2.00 indicated miles, and so we want the allowed time at 29.27 miles:

29.27 R/S displays: 29.27 (miles)
                            56.28 (minutes)
                            10.0317 (clock time)

We leave the 29.27-mile point at the indicated time, get back up to speed and make more time checks at 30 and 31 miles. The T in instruction 6 turns up at 31.99 miles. We effect the speed change as before:

31.99 R/S displays: 31.99 (miles
                            60.90 (minutes)
                            10.0754 (clock time)
43.2 STO 2   Stores new speed in R_2

We continue making regular time checks until we reach the stop sign in instruction 7, where our odometer reads 38.78 miles. Here we change speed to 24 mph:

38.78 R/S displays: 38.78 (miles)
                            70.30 (minutes)
                            10.1718 (clock time)
24 STO 2   Stores new speed in R_2

---

*Applies to Program II as well. When using Program I, use GTO 10 R/S. (This difference is noted in the program instruction summaries in the Appendix.)

Knowing that we have 6.02 miles to go at the new speed, we add that distance to 38.78 and see that the right turn and the speed change called for by instruction 7 will take place at 44.80 miles by our odometer.

We continue making a time check each mile up to 44 miles. Since the speed is slow, we have ample opportunity to anticipate instruction 8, which orders us to turn left at 45.67 miles from the start of the rally. To find the indicated distance we press 45.67 RCL 5 × and get 45.83 miles—and make a note.

At 44.80 miles we turn right and change speed to 34.5 mph:

44.8 R/S displays:	44.80 (miles)
	85.30 (minutes)
	10.3218 (clock time)
34.5 STO 2	Stores new speed in R_2

We check our time at 45 miles, turn left at 45.83 miles and are now ready to gain 40 seconds as required by instruction 9:

45.83 R/S displays:	45.83 (miles)
	87.08 (minutes)
	10.3405 (clock time)
.4 g H CHS GTO 11 R/S displays:	45.83 (miles)
	86.41 (minutes)
	10.3325 (clock time)

The time in R_0 has been shortened by 0.67 minute, and the time in R_7 by 40 seconds. We put our foot down in order to accomplish the gain within the allotted 4 miles; that is, before 49.67 official miles, or 49.84 odometer miles. To find the time we are due at the end of this 4-mile free zone:

49.84 R/S displays:	49.84 (miles)
	93.36 (minutes)
	10.4022 (clock time)

We manage that one on time and continue to make regular time checks while looking for the T in instruction 10. We find it at 54.08 miles:

54.08 R/S displays:	54.08 (miles)
	100.71 (minutes)
	10.4743 (clock time)
RCL 2 10 g % − STO 2	Stores the new speed, 31.05 mph, in R_2

55 R/S displays: 55.00 (miles)
  102.48 (minutes)
  10.4929 (clock time)

Watching now for the red barn in instruction 11, we complete 56 miles, 57 miles, 58 miles ... dead on time at every R/S and saying to ourselves, "Too bad there isn't a checkpoint right here." As we round the next bend in the road, at 58.60 miles, our wish is fulfilled; the control is in sight. Our practiced eye tells us that it is about five hundred feet ahead, about a tenth of a mile. While our driver holds his speed we quickly key in a pair of final checks:

58.65 R/S displays: 58.65 (miles)
  109.51 (minutes)
  10.5631 (clock time)
58.7 R/S displays: 58.70 (miles)
  109.61 (minutes)
  10.5636 (clock time)

At that mileage and at that instant we cross the timing line.

As soon as the checkpoint workers have timed us in and entered our arrival time—10:56.61—on our scorecard, they present us with a summary sheet containing the official figures for this leg:

	Average speed	Official distance	Total distance	Allowed time	Total time
Odometer check	32.00	20.00	20.00	37.500	37.500
	32.00	5.00	25.00	9.375	46.875
				2.300	49.175
Pause	35.2	6.88	31.88	11.727	60.902
	43.2	6.76	38.64	9.389	70.291
	24.00	6.00	44.64	15.000	85.291
				−0.667	84.624
Gain	34.50	9.25	53.89	16.087	100.711
	31.05	4.61	58.50	8.908	109.619

Time allowed: 109.62 minutes

To our dismay it appears that we failed to zero the checkpoint after all. We have incurred a one-point penalty, our elapsed time being 109.61 minutes. Did we err somewhere? Pressing RCL 6 shows our equivalent of the official distance to be correct: 58.50 miles. Not that one point is a bad score, but what happened?

The explanation is that we have been done in, if only by nine-thousandths of a minute, by the ubiquitous and inevitable vagaries of rounding. They occur more often than you might suspect; and since they tend to get buried under a lot of other uncertainties inherent in rallying they are more than likely to be overlooked. Fortunately, they are usually minuscule and negligible. Bear in mind that this sample rally was a long one, almost sixty miles on the road and almost two hours in duration. In real rallies, where checkpoints are generally closer together and leg times shorter, such quirks are apt to be of no moment.

It can reasonably be argued that the rallymaster here should have declared the allowed time to be 109.61 minutes, on the theory that you are not early (or late either) if you arrive within the hundredth-of-a-minute time slot in which you are due. He can counter, just as rationally, by saying that he is compelled to draw the line *somewhere* and that 109.62 is nearer to 109.619 than is 109.61. The point is moot and scarcely worth debating. What *is* certain is that a one-point penalty is a very creditable score.

If we had finished with a significant penalty but without having gone off course or made any other detectable mistakes, it is possible that our correction factors were slightly inaccurate. We might have misread the odometer at the end of the odometer check, or maybe our tires expanded or contracted along the way. Although we can do nothing about the leg just finished, we can refine our factor for the next leg. This we do by treating the whole first leg as an odometer check.

Suppose we had come in with 58.90 miles showing on our odometer instead of 58.70, and with a correspondingly painful time error. Pressing RCL 6 shows that the official distance we have accumulated in R_6 is 58.69 miles, whereas the summary sheet gives the official distance as 58.50 miles. Accordingly, we calculate a new Factor A: 58.5 ENTER 58.9 ÷ STO 4 writes it over the old Factor A in R_4. Then *g* 1/*x* STO 5 writes the new Factor B in R_5.

The new Factor A is 0.993208829; the original one was 0.996512207. The difference, barely 33 ten-thousandths of a mile (about 17 feet 5 inches), is not great, but of course it is additive. Since we cannot account for our problem in any other way, a new, refined set of factors is worth trying.

Of our not-to-be maligned one-point score you may say, "Very good. The calculations all came smoothly and accurately, and we did well. But we made no mistakes. How can the HP-25 help us when we goof?" The next chapter answers that question.

Chapter 6
Unmaking Mistakes

Recovering After Getting Lost

STRAYING MORE THAN a very short distance from the official course will more than likely ruin your score not only for that leg but for the whole rally. Still, you never know; recovery is sometimes possible. If you don't go down the wrong road too far, if you can find your way back, if the average speed is not too high, if the checkpoint is a fair distance ahead, you may be able to make up the lost time. A lot of if's, but as long as hope springs eternal, rallyists will make the effort.

The time that is lost when the way is lost builds up relentlessly. At an average speed of only 30 mph, going half a mile in the wrong direction costs one minute; getting turned around and driving back to the point of error doubles the loss, more or less. If you can average 40 mph on regaining the right road you will need four miles—six minutes—to catch up. If the average speed is high and if you have lost many minutes, odds are that the case is hopeless.

In the meantime your odometer is inflated by twice the distance you drove before discovering that you had gone astray. If the route instructions identify an upcoming action point in terms of official distance, you really have some figuring to do while your driver is struggling to make up for lost time. Under these trying conditions it would not take much to get you lost again. Hence the well-known advice: never make a turn (or fail to make a turn) until you are certain of your way. Making sure may waste a few moments, but it keeps the odds in your favor. Every rallyists knows that, of course; but the worst sometimes happens, and that is what this chapter is about.

To see what the HP-25 can do to help straighten out distorted time and mileage resulting from an off-course excursion, let's tackle a hypothetical rally leg for which this is the first instruction:

Start at 2:48 p.m. The average speed is 32.4 mph. At 7.77 miles turn left.

This time let's use Program I. Enter it (in PRGM mode), then switch to RUN and make the data entries. (At the end of the 20.20-mile odometer check our odometer read 20.44.)

32.4 STO 2
60 STO 3
20.2 ENTER 20.44 ÷ STO 4
g 1/x STO 5
f PRGM

Our odometer zeroed, at 2:48 we start our stopwatch and take off. As we make time checks at 1 mile (1.83 min.), 2 miles (3.66 min.) and 3 miles (5.49 min.) we seem to be progressing swimmingly. Anticipating the end of the fourth mile, we press 4 R/S—and at that moment we are dismayed to discover that we are on a road that has changed to dirt—and there are supposed to be no dirt roads in this rally. Somewhere back there we made a wrong turn—or failed to make the right one. Our nonreversing odometer reads 3.89 miles. We make a note.

Quickly we turn around and go back—the same way we came, of course—to the place where we made our mistake. The odometer now reads 4.46 miles. Since we cannot adjust the mileage in the odometer, the alternative is to adjust the allowed running time in the calculator. Regardless of how much time we have actually wasted in milling about, tearing our hair and cursing, all that concerns the calculator is the time allowed for the total off-course distance at the required average speed. If we have lost less than that, we are lucky; if more, we shall have to work harder to recover. In any case, some calculations are in order:

4.46 R/S displays: 4.46 (miles)
                    8.16 (minutes)

The "on-time" time for 4.46 miles, 8.16 minutes, must now be reduced by the off-course time:

4.46 ENTER 3.89 −   Half the off-course
                      distance = 0.57

2 ×   Total off-course
                      distance = 1.14 miles
*CHS GTO 04 R/S displays: 4.46 (miles)
                              6.08 (minutes)

This last operation calculates the negative value (−2.08 minutes) of the corrected time lost off course and adds it to R_0, effectively reducing the contents of R_0 without affecting the distance stored in R_1.

As you surely have perceived, the procedure to correct for time lost off course is similar to the one used for gain-time instructions except that the off-course routine uses the program to calculate the amount of time to be deducted.

Back on the right road now, late but hopeful, we have one more concern—to find out what our odometer is going to read at 7.77 official miles. Since the indicated distance in R_1 is inflated by 1.14 miles, we must add that "lost" mileage to our odometer equivalent of 7.77 official miles. First we convert 7.77 official miles to odometer miles, using Factor B from R_5; then we add our off-course distance:

7.77 ENTER RCL 5 × 1.14 +

The answer displayed tells us that the left turn will come up at 9.00 odometer miles.

If our car were equipped with a reversible or settable odometer, and if we chose to take advantage of it, the drill to compensate for our deviation down the garden path would be different. Using a reversible (subtracting) odometer, on discovering our mistake we would switch the instrument to − (subtract) and retrace our way to the point where we departed from the straight and narrow. It would now read 3.32 miles, which is just what it read when we erred. Then we would switch the odometer control back to + (add) and go.

In the case of a settable odometer we would calculate the reading where we erred, by subtracting 0.57 from 3.89, and set the instrument to read 3.32.

---

*For Programs II and III: CHS GTO 05 R/S.

In neither instance would it be necessary to adjust the time in the calculator.

The rule, then, is that if you cannot adjust your odometer for off-course distance, you must correct your time; but if you can, and do, correct your odometer, you must not correct your time.

Changing Speed at the Wrong Place

If it is possible to take a wrong turn owing to having misread or misinterpreted a route instruction or misidentified a landmark, it is equally possible to execute a speed change at the wrong place. You can compensate for such a mistake if you have made notes along the way. If there is the slightest doubt, make a note; if there is no doubt, make a note anyway. Assume this instruction:

Your average speed is 42 mph. At a dilapidated house on your left change average speed to 39 mph.

At 10.55 miles by your odometer you observe on your left a somewhat run-down residential structure and change speed there. Going along at the new speed, you presently espy on your left a domicile so dramatically decrepit that it makes the previous shack look like a palace. This *must* be the dilapidated house the rallymaster meant. Before exchanging opinions with your driver about the character of a rallymaster who would stoop to write such a subjective instruction, you jot down your odometer reading at this critical juncture: 13.75 miles.

What to do? Reconstruct, that's what—and press on, because for the past 3.2 miles you have been driving 3 mph too slow. The reconstruction is easy:

10.55 R/S	Restores to R_0 and R_1 the allowed time and the distance they contained when you changed speed
42 STO 2	Stores the correct speed in R_2
13.75 R/S	Calculates and displays the correct allowed time at 13.75 miles
39 STO 2	Effects the speed change at the proper place

As it happens, you are lucky; having lost only 0.35 minute (subject to your correction factor), your chances of recovering 21 seconds are good—unless the checkpoint is around the next bend.

Now that you know how to handle a speed change made too soon, you can deduce the remedy for a speed change *missed*. It might happen with a pair of instructions like these:

Your average speed is 38 mph. Turn
right at T.

When you turn onto Smith Road change
average speed to 28 mph.

You turn right at the T and continue to motor along at 38 mph. Being an astute rallyist determined to provide for all contingencies, you note your odometer reading at the T: 8.68 miles. Less astutely, however, you neglect to take a good look around the intersection. . . .

You check your time for 9 miles, 10 miles—and right about here you spot a sign revealing that the road you are on *is* Smith Road. Back at the T is where you should have changed speed to 28 mph. "Throw out the anchor!" you tell your driver, because you are now early, and the checkpoint may be around the next corner. Silently castigating the rallymaster for his deviousness and yourself for your inattention at the T, you set about repairing the damage:

8.68 R/S	Restores to R_0 and R_1 the allowed time and the distance they contained at the T
28 STO 2	Stores the correct speed in R_2
10 R/S	Calculates and displays the corrected allowed time where you are now

Check your watch and press on—discreetly.

When You've Pressed the Wrong Button

Keystroke mistakes, if detected in time, usually can be corrected without difficulty before any harm is done. You should develop the habit of always verifying number entries by reading the display. If you have pressed a wrong key, simply press CLx and start over. If you have gone too far, keying in some function before becoming aware of the error, f LASTx will restore the previous value in R_x and give you the opportunity to change it. The HP-25 Owner's Handbook explains in some detail how to correct keystroke mistakes including errors made in storing automatic programs.

If you commit some gross blunder that you believe to be disastrous (accidentally switching the power OFF is such a one—it promptly fills all sixty-one storage registers with big fat zeros), you will have to go back toward, and very likely all the way to, the beginning. This means reentering the program and all the associated data and then performing all the operations needed to restore the calculator to the condition it was in before you did your bad thing—in short, total reconstruction. It can be done easily and quickly, *provided* you have made notes.

"He wins at chess who makes the last mistake but one," a precept as old as that ancient game itself, has no meaning in rallying. In a rally a small mistake at the wrong time can plunge you instantly into last-place ignominy; and it is no use your hoping that everyone else will make the same or a worse mistake, because there is always at least one crew who will do everything right and airily profess to wonder how you could possibly have gone wrong. On the other hand, a massive error may not prove fatal. Not all tales of contestants who got so hopelessly lost that they packed up their gear and struck out for home only to stumble into the next checkpoint, incur a negligible penalty and ultimately collect a trophy are apocryphal; it once happened to this writer. That may be beside the point, but the moral is that there is always hope and that your chances of recovering from a colossal miscue are improved immeasurably if you have data to work with. Your calculator will calculate just about anything—if you have the figures to feed it. So take notes—copious notes. Some grains of graphite on a scrap of paper may turn out to be worth many times their weight in silver.

Chapter 7
Rally Scoring
Programs for the HP-25

HAVING SEEN HOW adeptly the HP-25 works for rally contestants, you may well wonder what it can do for rally organizers; they have their problems too, the most onerous of which is scoring, a chore that frequently outlasts the awards dinner's dessert and the contestants' patience.

Since scoring a rally consists mainly of performing, over and over again, the same calculations on series of different numbers, it is a process eminently suited to a programmable calculator, which never gets bored, tired or irritable. What is needed is a system that will store the constants (the allowed running time for each rally leg), accept the variables (each car's starting and finishing time for each leg), calculate the time actually taken, compare it with the time allowed, calculate the leg scores in penalty points, accumulate them and come up with each car's total score. If there is a maximum penalty for being late, that should be taken into account.

For the HP-25 all this is not only possible but easy. It is easy for the scorer as well; the principal demand of him is that he sit with the calculator, key in the start and finish times recorded on the scorecards, and press a few buttons to initialize and run the program.

HP-25 SCORING PROGRAM I

Scores one car at a time for up to seven legs at one point per second early or late (no maximum penalty.)

00			11	3
01	CHS		12	6
02	gH		13	0
03	x⇌y		14	0
04	gH		15	×
05	+		16	fPAUSE
06	x⇌y		17	fPAUSE
07	gH		18	gABS
08	+		19	STO + 0
09	f H.MS		20	GTO 00
10	gH			

Data Entries

Store the allowed time for leg 1 in R_1, the time for leg 2 in R_2, etc., for as many as seven legs. HP-25 notation requires that each time be keyed in as hours, decimal point, minutes and seconds. An allowed time for leg 1 of 1 hr. 15 min. 12 sec. would be entered at 1.1512 STO 1. An allowed time for leg 2 of 40 min. 4 sec. would be entered as .4004 STO 2.

Program Initialization

1. fPRGM   sets calculator to program step 00

2. fFIX 0   displays the scores in whole numbers without trailing zeros after the decimal point

3. RCL 1   recalls the allowed time for leg 1 from R_1 to R_x (no values to the right of the decimal point will be displayed, but they are of course preserved and used in the computations)

4. Key in Car 1's starting time for leg 1 as hours, decimal point, minutes and seconds (if any) and press ENTER. A starting time of 10:01:00 would be entered as 10.01 ENTER. (Times after noon must be expressed in 24-hour notation; 1:24:34 P.M. would be entered as 13.2434.)
5. Key in Car 1's finishing time for leg 1 in the same manner and press R/S. This first run of the program calculates Car 1's score of leg 1 at one point per second early or late; displays it as a positive number if the car was early, as a negative number if the car was late; stores the score as a positive value in R_0; then sends the calculator back to program step 00. The calculator is now ready to be initialized for leg 2.
6. Press RCL 2.
7. Key in Car 1's leg 2 starting time and press ENTER.
8. Key in Car 1's leg 2 finishing time and press R/S. The second run calculates the score for leg 2, displays it and adds it to the leg 1 score stored in R_0.
9. Repeat this procedure for up to seven legs. When the program has been run for the final leg, press RCL 0 to display Car 1's total point score. Record the score *and clear* R_0 *by pressing* 0 STO 0. Note that it is not necessary to press CLx or f STK. Do not in any case press f REG; that would clear all the allowed leg times for the memory registers. The calculator is now ready to score Car 2.

How the Basic Scoring Program Works

In order to manipulate the allowed, starting and finishing times efficiently and in that order, this program—like the three others that follow—relies on exploiting the HP-25 stack. The object is to begin with the three times lodged, respectively, in R_z, R_y and R_x and subsequently to retrieve the contents of R_y and R_z into R_x by means of the $x \rightleftarrows y$ exchange key. Therefore our formula for calculating the time error is:

$- \text{(finish time)} + \text{(start time)} + \text{(allowed time)}$
$\qquad\qquad\qquad\qquad\qquad = error$ in decimal hours.

Then: *error* $\times 360 = penalty\ points$.

At program step 00, after initialization, the contents of the stack are:

R_t inconsequential (actually, R_t contains the last allowed time stored in a memory; this value will float in the stack, not descending into R_x)

R_z allowed time

R_y start time

R_x finish time

Step 01 gives the finish time a negative sign. Step 02 converts the hours-minutes-seconds finish time to decimal hours. Step 03 brings the hours-minutes-seconds start time into R_x, placing the converted negative finish time in R_y. Step 04 converts the start time to decimal hours. Step 05 algebraically adds these two times, giving the time taken in negative decimal hours. Now R_y contains the hours-minutes-seconds allowed time; step 06 brings this value into R_x, parking the time taken in R_y. Step 07 converts the allowed time to decimal hours. Step 08 adds this value to the negative value in R_y. R_x now contains the time error in decimal hours.

Steps 09 and 10 serve as somewhat obscure purpose. The HP-25's conversion between hours-minutes-seconds and decimal hours being accurate to only five decimal places, certain combinations of start, finish and allowed times that should produce a zero error will leave a random value other than zero in the ninth decimal place after step 08 is executed. This number multiplied by 3600 (steps 11–15) will deposit a value other than zero in R_0 at step 19. Steps 09 and 10, in spite of their apparent redundancy, effectively eliminate the unwanted value.

Steps 11–15 multiply the decimal-hours error by 3600 (1 point per second = 3600 points per hour). Steps 16–17 display the point score for recording—positive if early, negative if late. Step 18 renders a negative point score positive. Step 19 adds the positive point score into R_0. Step 20 returns the calculator to step 00.

To familiarize yourself with the routine, try practicing with these data for Car 1 in a four-leg event:

Allowed times	hrs	min	sec
Leg 1	1	15	12
Leg 2		40	04
Leg 3		51	10
Leg 4	1	03	00

Car 1's scorecard:

Leave start	10	01	00
Arrive checkpoint 1	11	10	20
Leave checkpoint 1	11	13	00
Arrive checkpoint 2	11	54	09
Leave checkpoint 2	11	57	00
Arrive checkpoint 3	13	01	59
Leave checkpoint 3	13	04	30
Arrive checkpoint 4	14	07	30

Enter the program, store the allowed times, initialize the program and run it through the four sets of scorecard times. The penalties are: leg 1, 352 early; leg 2, 65 late; leg 3, 829 late; leg 4, 0; total 1,246.

This program is all right, you say, except that your club, as many clubs do in order to discourage frantic and possibly risky attempts to recover time lost on the road, sets a maximum point penalty for lateness. Very well, let's work on that problem.

It is clear that we shall have to make some tests and branch the program according to their results. We must persuade the calculator to determine whether the car was early or late at each checkpoint. If it was early, the calculator should impose the full one-point-per-second penalty. If it was late, the calculator will have to find out whether it was more than so many minutes late. (We will assume a five-minute maximum here, but the figure can be whatever club policy dictates.) If so, only the maximum penalty is imposed; if not, the penalty is calculated in full at one point per second. The somewhat sophisticated program wanted comes out like this:

HP-25 MAXIMUM-PENALTY SCORING PROGRAM IA

Scores one car at a time for up to seven legs at one point per second early or late with a maximum penalty for lateness of 5 minutes or 300 points

```
00
01  CHS           06  x⇄y
02  gH            07  gH
03  x⇄y           08  +
04  gH            09  f H.MS
05  +             10  gH
```
(continued on page 92)

(cont. from previous page)

11	g x ⩾ 0	23	3
12	GTO 23	24	6
13	ENTER	25	0
14	ENTER	26	0
15*	.	27	×
16	0	28	f PAUSE
17	5	29	f PAUSE
18	gH	30	g ABS
19	+	31	STO + 0
20	gx ⩾ 0	32	GTO 00
21	GTO 33	33	R ↓
22	f LASTx	34	GTO 23

Normally it is unnecessary to key in a trailing zero, but it must be done here in order to keep the number of program steps at 34.

The data entries and program initialization are made exactly as under the basic scoring program. Test the new program using the same Car 1 allowed times and starting and finishing times. The total score, displayed when you finally press RCL 0, will now be 717 points.

You will find it instructive, perhaps even entertaining, to analyze this program step by step. Steps 01–10 calculate the time error exactly as in the previous program. The test at step 11 asks whether the error is equal to or greater than zero. If the answer is yes, the car was either early or on time and should receive the score it has actually earned. Thus the calculator goes to the next step (12), which sends it to step 23. Steps 23–27 multiply the time value, which is in decimal hours, by 3600, converting it to seconds. Steps 28–29 display the time error for recording purposes. Steps 30–31 add the penalty points into R_0, and step 32 returns the calculator to step 00.

If the answer to the test at step 11 is no (time error less than zero, or negative), the car was late. Now the calculator must determine whether it was less or more than 5 minutes late. Skipping

---

*The number .05 in steps 15–17 is the limit of late time to be scored, in this case 5 minutes (300 points). Note that if the limit were 10 minutes the entry would have to be keyed in this way:

15 .
16 1
17 0 (or g NOP)

automatically to step 13, the calculator places the time taken in R_y and, in step 14, in R_z also; this is a parking operation. Steps 15–18 convert 5 minutes to its decimal-hour equivalent (0.083333333 hr.), and step 19 adds this value to the time taken, which, remember, is negative. Step 20 asks whether the algebraic sum is equal to or greater than zero. If the answer is yes, the car was not more than 5 minutes late and should receive the point score earned. Step 21 sends the calculator to step 33, which rolls down the time error into R_x. Step 34 sends the calculator to step 23. Steps 23–31 calculate the point score, display its negative value and add its positive value into R_0. Step 32 sends the calculator back to step 00.

If the answer to the test at step 20 is no, the car was no more than 5 minutes late and must be given only the maximum point score The calculator skips to step 22, which retrieves the previous x—the decimal-hour equivalent of 5 minutes. Steps 23–27 multiply that by 3600. Steps 28–29 display 300 points. Step 30 has no effect in this case. Step 31 stores the score, and step 32 returns the calculator to step 00.

A neat enough routine, you say, but useless where a rally is to be timed and scored in minutes and hundredths of minutes, as is customary nowadays. That presents a problem, because the HP-25 can deal with times expressed in hours, minutes and seconds, or in minutes and seconds, or in minutes and hundredths of minutes, but not in hours, minutes and hundredths of minutes—not, at least, without some persuasion. The trick is to change hours and decimal minutes, which it will not handle, to plain decimal minutes, which it will. This calls for slightly more elaborate program.

The conversion is made in three stages. First the minutes and hundredths component, contained in the first four places following the decimal point, is multiplied by 100. Then the hours component, which occupies the one or two places at the left of the decimal point, is multiplied by 60. Finally, the two products are added. For example, a starting time of 9:30.25 (30 1/4 minutes past 9 o'clock) is keyed into the calculator as 9.3025. Multiplying .3025 by 100 gives 30.25 minutes. Multiplying 9 by 60 gives 540 minutes. Adding the two gives 570.25 minutes, a form that the calculator will handle as an ordinary number. By the same token, a finishing time of 10:02.17, keyed in as 10.0217, becomes 602.17 minutes. The time taken is 602.17 − 570.25, or 31.92 minutes. If the time allowed is 31.89

minutes, the car is .03 minute late, and multiplying .03 by 100 gives the point score, 3.

The HP-25 will handily make these conversions with the help of two keyboard functions designated in Chapter 1 as not ordinarily used in rally work. They are the blue-function FRAC (fraction) and the gold-function INT (integer). To see how they work, key in 9.3025 and press *g* FRAC. The 9 vanishes, leaving only the fractional part. (Fix 4 decimal places to observe the effect better.) Key in 100 ×. The answer is 30.2500 minutes. Reenter 9.3025 and press *f* INT. Now the fraction disappears, leaving 9.0000. Key in 60 ×. The answer is 540.0000 minutes. Now keying in 30.25 + displays 570.2500 minutes.

A crude demonstration, to be sure. In practice it is not necessary to key in a time twice. You can duplicate it in the stack and roll it back down into the display when you need it the second time. The more polished routine is this:

Keystrokes	*Effect*
9.3025	9.3025 in R_x
ENTER	9.3025 in R_x and R_y
g FRAC	0.3025
100 ×	30.25 in R_x
STO 0	30.25 stored in R_0
R↓	9.3025 drops into R_x
f INT	9. in R_x
60 ×	540 in R_x
STO + 0	570.25 in R_0

This scheme is easily built into a program that will handle hours-minutes-hundredths scoring.

HP-25 SCORING PROGRAM II

Scores one car at a time for up to six legs at one point per hundredth of a minute early or late (no maximum penalty for lateness)

00		07	ENTER
01	R↓	08	*g* FRAC
02	R↓	09	EEX
03	STO 0	10	2
04	R↓	11	×
05	R↓	12	STO + 0
06	CHS	13	R↓

14	*f* INT	24	*f* PAUSE
15	6	25	*g* ABS
16	0	26	EEX
17	×	27	2
18	STO + 0	28	×
19	*g* x<0	29	STO + 7
20	GTO 32	30	*f* FIX 0
21	RCL 0	31	GTO 00
22	*f* FIX 2	32	R↓
23	*f* PAUSE	33	GTO 08

Data Entries

Store the allowed time for leg 1 in R_1 *as minutes, decimal point, hundredths of minutes,* the allowed time for leg 2 in R_2, and so on for as many as six legs. (R_0 is used in the calculations, and R_7 is used to sum the penalty points.) Allowed times longer than one hour must be keyed in as decimal minutes; *e.g.*, 1 hr. 8 1/2 min. would be keyed in as 68.5 STO *n*.

Program Initialization

1. *f* PRGM   Sets the calculator to program step 00

2. RCL 1   Recalls the allowed time for leg 1 from R_1 and displays it to two decimal places only; the complete decimal part, however, is preserved for calculating purposes

3. Key in Car 1's starting time for leg 1 *as hours, decimal point, minutes and hundredths* and press ENTER.
4. Key in Car 1's finishing time for leg 1 in the same way and press R/S. The time error will be displayed at steps 23–24 in minutes and hundredths—positive if the car was early, negative if late, zero if on time. The leg score in penalty points will be displayed at step 31, always as a positive value.
5. Contine the procedure for as many as six legs. Be warned that, in scoring legs 2, 3, 4, 5 and 6, when you press RCL

n, the display of the allowed time may be confusing. If the allowed time contains a fraction in addition to a whole number (*i.e.*, hundredths of minutes in addition to minutes), the display will be rounded to the nearest integer; *e.g.*, 63.25 minutes will appear as 63. The reason is that step 30 fixes the point-score display (step 31) at zero decimal places. The fractional value at the right of the decimal point is nevertheless preserved for calculating purposes.

6. When the last leg has been scored, pressing RCL 7 will display the car's total score. Record the score *and press* 0 STO 7 *to clear* R_7. The calculator is now ready to score Car 2.

If there is a maximum penalty for lateness, the program that follows will take care of it.

HP-25 MAXIMUM-PENALTY SCORING PROGRAM IIA

Scores one car at a time for up to six legs at one point per hundredth of a minute early or late with a maximum penalty for lateness of 5 minutes or 500 points

00		19	$g\ x < 0$
01	R↓	20	GTO 34
02	R↓	21	RCL 0
03	STO 0	22	f FIX 2
04	R↓	23	f PAUSE
05	R↓	24	f PAUSE
06	CHS	25	$g\ x < 0$
07	ENTER	26	GTO 36
08	g FRAC	27	EEX
09	EEX	28	2
10	2	29	×
11	×	30	g ABS
12	STO + 0	31	STO + 7
13	R↓	32	f FIX 0
14	f INT	33	GSO 00
15	6	34	R↓
16	0	35	GTO 07
17	×	36	ENTER
18	STO + 0		

37 ENTER	42 GTO 45
38 0	43 f LASTx
39 5	44 GTO 27
40 +	45 R↓
41 g x≥0	46 GTO 27

Data entries and program initilization for Scoring Program IIA are exactly the same as those for Scoring Program II.

As with Program IA, the limit of lateness illustrated is 5 minutes; however, the time limit keyed in at steps 38 – 39 can be any number of whole minutes from 01 to 99.

To test these two programs, try these time data for a five-leg event:

Allowed times	minutes and hundredths	store as
Leg 1	47.98	47.98 STO 1
Leg 2	21.00	21 STO 2
Leg 3	63.25	63.25 STO 3
Leg 4	31.07	31.07 STO 4
Leg 5	36.20	36.2 STO 5

Car 1's scorecard

Leave start	11:01.00
Arrive checkpoint 1	11:48.90
Leave checkpoint 1	11:51.00
Arrive checkpoint 2	12:12.12
Leave checkpoint 2	12:15.00
Arrive checkpoint 3	13:25.00
Leave checkpoint 3	14:31.00
Arrive checkpoint 4	14:57.04
Leave checkpoint 4	15:00.50
Arrive checkpoint 5	15:36.70

	Scoring Displays	
Keystrokes	*Program II*	*Program IIA*
f PRGM		
RCL 1		
11.01 ENTER		
11.489 R/S	0.08 (min.)	0.08 (min.)
	8. (points)	8. (points)

cont. on next page

	Scoring Displays	
Keystrokes	Program II	Program IIA
RCL 2		
11.51 ENTER		
12.1212 R/S	− 0.12 (min.)	− 0.12 (min.)
	12. (points)	12. (points)
RCL 3		
12.15 ENTER		
13.25 R/S −	− 6.75 min.	− 6.75 min.
	675. (points)	500. (points)
RCL 4		
14.31 ENTER		
14.5704 R/S	5.03 (min.)	5.03 (min.)
	503. (points)	503. (points)
RCL 5		
15.005 ENTER		
15.367 R/S	0.00 (min.)	0.00 (min.)
	0. (points)	0. (points)
RCL 7	1198. (points)	1023 (points)
0 STO 7		

* * *

Possibly you prefer to score checkpoint by checkpoint instead of car by car; that is, you want to score all the cars for Leg 1, then all the cars for Leg 2, and so on. Furthermore, your club's rules may, like those currently governing Sports Car Club of America national and divisional rallies, prescribe a five-minute maximum for earliness as well as for lateness. If so, this program will meet your requirements:

HP-25 CHECKPOINT-BY-CHECKPOINT SCORING PROGRAM III

Scores one leg at a time at a one point per hundredth of a minute early or late with a flat maximum penalty of 5 minutes or 500 points

00
01   CHS
02   ENTER
03   *g* FRAC

cont. on next page

04	EEX	23	ENTER
05	2	24	ENTER
06	×	25	5
07	STO + 0	26	−
08	R↓	27	g x <0
09	f INT	28	GTO 38
10	6	29	f LASTx
11	0	30	EEX
12	×	31	2
13	STO + 0	32	×
14	g x<0	33	0
15	GTO 40	34	STO 0
16	RCL 0	35	R↓
17	RCL 1	36	f FIX 0
18	+	37	GTO 00
19	f FIX 2	38	R↓
20	f PAUSE	39	GTO 30
21	f PAUSE	40	R↓
22	g ABS	41	GTO 02

HP-25 Scoring Program III

Data Entry

Store in R_1 the allowed time for the leg to be scored as minutes, decimal point, hundredths of minutes. For example, an allowed time of 37.54 minutes would be keyed in as 37.54 STO 1. An allowed time of 1 hr. 2.08 minutes would be keyed in as 62.08 STO 1.

Program Initialization

1. f PRGM
2. Key in the car's starting time as hours, decimal point, minutes and hundredths and press ENTER. A starting time of 1:04.00 p.m. would be keyed in as 13.04 ENTER.
3. Key in the car's finishing time in the same way and press R/S. The program run calculates the time error and displays it (steps 20–21) in minutes and hundredths (with a negative sign if the car was late); the second display (step 37) gives the point score.

4. To score the next car, go back to initialization step 2.
5. To score the next leg, store the allowed time in R₁ and proceed to initialization step 2.

To test Program III, assume an allowed time for Leg 1 of 27.84 minutes; key in 27.84 STO 1 *f* PRGM

		Displays
Car 1 start time	9:01.00	− 0.20
Car 1 finish time	9:29.04	20
Car 2 start time	9:02.00	1.67
Car 2 finish time	9:28.17	167
Car 3 start time	9:03.00	6.16
Car 3 finish time	9:24.68	500
Car 4 start time	9:04.00	− 5.52
Car 4 finish time	9:37.36	500
Car 5 start time	9:05.00	0.00
Car 5 finish time	9:32.84	0

THE TEXAS INSTRUMENTS SR-56
PROGRAMMABLE POCKET ELECTRONIC CALCULATOR

Part II
The Texas Instruments Pocket Calculator SR-56 Programmable

Chapter 8
Getting Acquainted with the SR-56

Programmability

THE SR-56 IS a *programmable* calculator. Once you have determined how to solve a mathematical problem with it manually, you can program it to solve the same problem, or a series of similar problems, over and over again *automatically*. The advantages that programmability offer you as a rally navigator are, it might be said, almost incalculable. Once you have stored the navigational program, you have only to key in the distance for which you want the corrected allowed driving time and press the run/stop key. The answer is displayed almost instantly.

You need not be a computer programmer to program and operate the SR-56; you don't have to know computer theory or learn a computer language. The SR-56 is keyboard programmed. Having switched it to "learn" mode, you press the keys in the same sequence as when you solved the problem manually. When you switch to "execute" mode and press the run/stop key, the calculator consults the string of instructions you have stored and executes this program using whatever numbers you have given it to work with. As soon as it has displayed the answer, it is ready to go again.

A Word About Algebraic Notation

Like the majority of pocket calculators, the SR-56 uses the computational system known as Algebraic Notation. Designers and manufacturers and sellers of AN calculators like to stress the point that, using their machines, you solve the problem "exactly as it is written, from left to right." That is true enough, but it is not the whole truth. Some mathematical expressions are neither written nor solved strictly from left to right—or even from top to bottom. Consider this series:

$$1 + \cfrac{1}{2 + \cfrac{1}{2 + \cfrac{1}{2 + \cfrac{1}{2 + 1 \ldots}}}}$$

This is an infinite sequence, and it must be attacked from somewhere down near the lower right-hand corner and worked from southeast to northwest. (Having climbed the staircase and crossed the top landing, you will perhaps be gratified to discover that the sequence gives a value very, very close to the square root of 2.)

On the whole, AN machines do perform the elementary arithmetic operations quite straightforwardly:

Keystrokes	Display
2	2
+	2.
3	3
=	5.
9	9
−	9.
6	6
=	3.
11	11
×	11.
99	99
=	1089.
48.65	48.65
÷	48.65
7.5	7.5
=	6.486666667

Chain calculations, too, are simple enough—up to a point:
$$4 + 5 - 3 = 6. \quad 90 \times 5 \div 6 = 75.$$

But this is about as far as multiple-term expressions can be taken without some forethought. Consider these three:

$$\frac{90 \times 5}{6} \qquad \frac{90}{6} \times 5 \qquad 90 \times \frac{5}{6}$$

They are for all purposes identical, all the same as $90 \times 5 \div 6$. However, such an expression as $90 \div 5 \times 6$ is meaningless. It must be written either as $(90 \div 5) \times 6$ or as $90 \div (5 \times 6)$; the answers are quite far apart: 108 and 3.

Consider this one: $3 + 4 \times 5 + 6 =$? As written, it too makes nought but nonsense; indeed, it is fascinating to discover that, worked from left to right on different types of calculators, it produces different answers.

Most inexpensive, basic four-function AN calculators handle it this way:

Keystrokes	Display
3 + 4	7
× 5 +	35
6 =	41

RPN calculators like the Hewlett-Packard family's give the same answer:

3 ENTER 4 +	7
5 ×	35
6 +	41

In both cases the calculators have treated the equation as if it had been written $((3 + 4) \times 5) + 6 = ?$ The SR-56, though, comes up with a different answer. It solves the equation as though it were written $3 + (4 \times 5) + 6$, and gives 29. The reason is that if parentheses are omitted, the SR-56 performs chained arithmetical operations in a predetermined sequence that accords with its built-in "algebraic hierarchy."

The thing of importance is that you have to write any equation or formula or other mathematical expression to suit the particular calculator you intend to use to solve it. If you are already reflecting that there are two other ways to write $3 + 4 \times 5 + 6$, and two other answers, you are right:

$$(3 + 4) \times (5 + 6) = 77$$
$$3 + (4 \times (5 + 6)) = 47$$

Parentheses, then, are the key to setting off the terms in a mathematical expression and to designating the order in which the arithmetical operations are to be performed. Parentheses (and brackets— [ ] —which serve the exact same purpose) are equally important to you whether you use an AN or an RPN calculator. Even though RPN calculators have no parentheses on their keyboards (no equals sign either), the parentheses written in the expression dictate the user's plan of attack. For example, using an RPN calculator to solve 3 + (4 × (5 + 6)), you would work from the inside out and, as a matter of fact, pretty much from right to left:

5 ENTER 6 + 4 × 3 + displays the answer, 47

Using the SR-56 and similar AN machines, your keystrokes would be these:

3 + (4 × (5 + 6 =

Here it is not necessary to key in the closing parentheses before pressing the = key; but you had better have sorted out the opening ones very carefully and have keyed them in at all the right places.

To sum up, the parentheses are (or ought to be) stated in the expression no matter what kind of calculator is in question. The differences are wholly among the calculators, and the essential difference between AN and RPN is that AN requires keying in parentheses, while RPN requires assessing the expression and deciding where to start solving it.

Among persons who use calculators a very great deal, prejudices pro and con AN and RPN can run strong. The question is not whether the one is "better" than the other. The choice is pure personal preference. Generally speaking, RPN calculators are somewhat easier to use, require fewer keystrokes and make do with fewer program steps. AN calculators, nevertheless, are perfectly adequate and give just as good right answers. That the SR-56 is a highly useful aid to average-speed rally navigation and to rally scoring there is no doubt whatsoever.

The Keyboard

It is hardly necessary to point out that the keyboard of an advanced calculator is not something you master in minutes. The SR-56 has forty keys, most of which perform more than one function. For purposes of identification and programming, the keys are numbered according to a somewhat modified matrix system. The x^2

key, for example, is designated key 43: fourth row from the top, third key from the left. Two-function keys have a number for each function; when the x^2 key is used for $\sqrt{x}$, its number is 48. The accompanying chart shows all the keycodes.

For perusal now and reference later, here are descriptions of what the keys do:

SR-56 PROGRAM KEYCODES

Key	Keycode	Key	Keycode	Key	Keycode	Key	Keycode	Key	Keycode
		INV	17	log	18	10^x	19	CLR	10
2nd	none	INV	12	ln$x$	13	e^x	14	CLR	15
f(n)	26	dsz	27	$\|x\|$	28	Int	29	1/x	20
LRN	none	GTO	22	sin	23	cos	24	tan	25
bst	none	$x=t$	37	CMs	38	EXC	39	PROD	30
SST	none	$x \leq t$	32	STO	33	RCL	34	SUM	35
NOP	46	$x \geq t$	47	$\sqrt{x}$	48	fix	49	$\sqrt[x]{y}$	40
R/S	41	RST	42	x^2	43	EE	44	y^x	45
CP	56	subr	57	rtn	58	pause	59		
CE	51	(	52	)	53	÷	54		
7	07	8	08	9	09	π	69		
7	07	8	08	9	09	×	64		
$\Sigma+$	04	$\Sigma-$	05	6	06	RAD	79		
4	04	5	05	6	06	−	74		
Mean	01	P→R	02	R→P	03				
1	01	2	02	3	03	+	84		
S. Dev.	00	prt	97	pap	98	list	99		
0	00	•	92	+/−	93	=	94		

SR-56 PROGRAM KEYCODES

(For clarity, most of the keycodes not used in the navigation and scoring programs have been omitted)

Keycode	Key	Keycode	Key	Keycode	Key	Keycode	Key
00	0	17	*INV	37	*$x = t$	54	÷
01	1	19	*10^x	38	*CMs	56	*CP
02	2	20	*$1/x$	39	*EXC	57	*subr
03	3	22	GTO	41	R/S	58	*rtn
04	4	28	* $\vert x \vert$	42	RST	59	*pause
05	5	29	*Int	46	*NOP	64	×
06	6	30	*PROD	47	*$x \geq t$	74	−
07	7	32	$x \leq t$	49	*fix	84	+
08	8	33	STO	51	CE	92	•
09	9	34	RCL	52	(	93	+/−
12	INV	35	SUM	53	)	94	=

2nd (no keycode): *Second function.* Accesses any of the second calculator functions printed in gold above first-function keys. For example, to find the reciprocal of the number displayed, press 2nd, then press the key directly below $1/x$, the tan (tangent) key. In the SR-56 Owner's Manual notation, this combination of keys is written *$1/x$. *Throughout this Part II, the asterisk is used to denote the SR-56's 2nd-function key.*

Note that if this key is pressed twice in succession, the calculator returns to first-function operation.

INV (keycode 12): *Inverse.* The Inverse key commands the inverse of certain first or second functions. For example, SUM 1 tells the calculator to add the value displayed in the x-register to the value stored in memoy R_1. INV SUM 1 tells it to *subtract* the x value from the R_1 value.

When used with second functions, INV may be pressed before or after the 2nd key: INV *Int has exactly the same effect as *INV Int. (The keycode for *INV is 17.)

If no other keys have been pressed, pressing INV a second time cancels the inverse command.

ln$x$ (keycode 18): *Natural logarithm.* Calculates the log to the base e of the number displayed.

*log (keycode 13): *Common logarithm.* Calculates the log to the base 10 of the number displayed.

---

*Denotes 2nd function key

e^x (keycode 14); *Natural antilogarithm.* Calculates the natural antilog of the number displayed.

*10ˣ (keycode 19): *Common antilogarithm.* Calculates the common antilog of the number displayed.

CLR (keycode 15) or *CLR (keycode 10): *Clear.* Clears not only the display but all calculations in progress. (Does not clear the memory registers, the program memory, the T-register, the subroutine level counter or the fixed-point mode.)

LRN (no keycode): *Learn.* Pressing the LRN key once puts the calculator in learn mode, allowing you to enter a program and store it in the 100-step program memory. Pressing LRN a second time takes the calculator out of learn mode. (The LRN key preserves the value displayed.)

*f(n) (keycode 26): This special function key accesses the six functions printed in blue in rows 7, 8 and 9 of the keyboard. It is not used in rally work.

GTO (keycode 22): *Go to.* GTO followed by a two-digit program-step address sends the calculator to that location. For example, in either calculate mode or execute (run-program) mode, GTO 09 sends the calculator to program step 09; in execute mode, the program will continue to run from there.

*dsz (keycode 27): *Decrement and skip on zero.* A combination counter and conditional transfer used in certain iterative programs. It is not used in any of the rally programs.

sin (keycode 23): *Sine.* A trigonometric function not used in the rally programs.

*| x | (keycode 28): *Absolute value.* Changes the sign of a negative number; leaves a positive number unchanged.

cos (keycode 24): *Cosine.* A trig function.

*Int (keycode 29): *Integer.* Discards the fractional part (all numbers to the right of the decimal point), leaving only the integer (whole-number) part. INV *Int discards the integer part and preserves the fraction.

These two truncating functions make possible the time conversions that are essential to some of the navigating programs and to all of the scoring programs.

tan (keycode 25): *Tangent.* Another trig function.

*1/x (keycode 20): *Reciprocal.* Divides 1 by the value in the display register.

SST (no keycode): *Single-step.* Increments the program counter by 1. In learn mode, it displays the next program storage location. In calculate mode, it executes the program one step at a time, displaying the result after each step has been performed.

*bst (no keycode): *Back-step.* Pressing this key, which operates in learn mode only, decrements the program counter by 1 and displays the corresponding program instruction code.

$x \leq t$ (keycode 32): $x - t$ *exchange.* Exchanges the value x in the display register for the value t in the T-register.

This key is used to set up certain tests in conditional program branching, as in the maximum-penalty rally scoring programs.

*$x = t$ (keycode 37): *"Is x equal to t?"* Asks whether the value displayed is equal to the value stored in the T-register. This is one of the tests used in conditional program branching.

If the answer to the question is yes, the calculator branches to the program-register whose address is stored in the two program steps that immediately follow. If the answer is no, the calculator bypasses the yes-answer address and proceeds to the next step.

(INV ***$x = t$** asks, *"Is x unequal to t?"*)

STO (keycode 33): *Store.* Pressing this key and then the number (0 to 9) of a memory register stores the x value in that memory. For example, 16 x^2 STO 6 stores 256 in R_6. A new value, including 0, can be stored in any memory at any time, overwriting the memory's previous content.

*CMs (keycode 38) *Clear memories.* Clears to zero all ten memory registers. Does not affect the internal processing registers, the display, the program memories, the T-register or the subroutine level counter.

RCL (keycode 34): *Recall.* Pressing RCL followed by a number key from 0 to 9 recalls and displays the content of the designated memory register. Recalling a value from memory does not clear the memory; the effect is merely to borrow, or copy, the value, which remains stored.

*EXC (keycode 39): *Memory/display exchange.* Pressing ***EXC** followed by a memory register number (0 to 9) exchanges the content of the display register with that of the designated memory register.

This ability to recall a stored value and to simultaneously replace it with a new value affords considerable convenience as well as economies of keystrokes and program steps. It is used extensively in the rally scoring programs for the effective manipulation of times, both whole and truncated.

SUM (keycode 35): *Add to memory*. Pressing SUM, then a number key from 0 to 9, adds the value in the display register to the value in the designated memory. The new value is stored in that memory; the value in the display register remains unchanged.

INV SUM: *Subtract from memory*. Pressing INV SUM n subtracts the value displayed from the value stored in R_n.

*PROD (keycode 30): *Multiply in memory*. Pressing *PROD n multiplies the content of R_n by the value displayed.

R/S (keycode 41): *Run/stop*. Pressing R/S stops a program that is running; or it starts (or restarts) the execution of a program at the step where the program counter is positioned.

An R/S instruction within a program halts program execution at that step until R/S is pressed again; thus it provides for a mid-program data entry or for a check on an intermediate result.

*NOP (keycode 46): *No operation*. In learn mode, *NOP deletes an unwanted program instruction or provides intervals between program parts for possible later insertions. When the calculator encounters a no-operation instruction it skips to the next program step.

RST (keycode 42): *Reset*. Instructs the calculator to reset the program counter to step 00. (It also sets the subroutine level counter to zero, but it does not affect the T-register.)

*$x \geq t$ (keycode 47): *"Is x equal to or greater than t?"* Asks whether the displayed value equals or exceeds the value in the T-register. Another conditional test.

(INV *$x \geq t$ asks, *"Is x less than t?"*)

x^2 (keycode 43): *x square*. Squares the number in the display register.

*$\sqrt{x}$ (keycode 48): *Square root of x*. Calculates the square root of the number (which must carry a positive sign) in the display register.

EE (keycode 44): *Scientific notation*. Used to key in, with an exponent, very large and very small numbers. Not used in any of the rally programs.

*fix (keycode 49): *Fix decimal point*. When first turned on, the calculator is in floating-point mode; that is, it will display from zero to ten decimal places, depending on the magnitude of the value in the x-register. To suit your own purposes you can round the display to any number of places from zero to eight. For example, *fix 4 fixes the number of places at four. Only the display is rounded; the undisplayed values are preserved and used in any subsequent calculations.

Note the nature of the floating and fixed decimals. Turn your SR-56 off, then on, perform the following operations and observe the display:

Keystrokes	Display
	0
1 ÷ 3 =	.3333333333
*fix 4	0.3333
*fix 2	0.33
*fix 1	0.3
*fix 0	0.

The round-down is now complete; but the fact that the complete fraction is preserved can be proved readily:

× 3 =	1.
*fix 8	1.00000000

At this point, by the way, lesser calculators would display 0.999999999. The SR-56, by using more digits internally (twelve or thirteen) than it displays (ten), rounds accurately to ten digits.

y^x (keycode 45): Raise y to the xth power, Key in y, press y^x, key in x, press =.

* $\sqrt[x]{y}$ (keycode 40): *Take the xth root of y.* Having keyed in y, press * $\sqrt[x]{y}$, key in x, press =.

CE (keycode 51): *Clear error.* Clears an incorrect number entry, including a decimal point entry, made from the keyboard. It does not clear results of calculations or recalled numbers or π. It will stop a flashing error display without affecting the number displayed or any pending calculations.

CE has another, altogether different use. When it is pressed immediately following a mathematical operator key, such as +, −, ×, ÷, (, and the log, power and root keys, it has the effect of reentering the value in the display register. These are examples of the keystroke economies that result:

$$978 + 978 = ?$$

Pressing 978 + CE = gives the answer without keying in 978 a second time.

$$\sqrt[99]{99} = ?$$

Press 99 $*\sqrt[x]{y}$ CE = to get the root: 1.047509406.

CE also serves to repeat an x-value and place it after an opening parenthesis:

$$16^2 + (16^2 + 8^2)^2 = ?$$

To avoid squaring 16 twice:

16 x^2 + (CE +8x^2) x^2 = gives the answer, 102656.

*x/y (keycode 40): Take the xth root of y. Press *x/y, enter x, press =.

CE (keycode 51): Clear error. Clears an incorrect number entry, including a decimal point entry, *made from the keyboard.* It does not clear results of calculations or recalled number or (π). It will stop a flashing error display without affecting the number displayed or any pending calculations.

((keycode 52): *Opening parenthesis.*
) (keycode 53): *Closing parenthesis.*

In algebraic notation, wherever a mathematical sequence cannot be handled directly by the single-function keys (trig, log, exponent, root, multiplication, division, addition, subtraction, equals), certain terms of the expression must be set off by parentheses. The SR-56 Owner's Manual devotes a dozen pages to algebraic hierarchy and the use of parentheses and the equals sign. They are worth your careful study. Here we can only sum up by pointing out that in some instances parentheses are compulsory (as you have already seen in the infamous case of 3 +4 × 5 + 6) and in others merely convenient. The convenience arises from the fact that every time the SR-56 encounters a closing parenthesis, it evaluates the expression back to the opening parenthesis and displays the value, helping you to keep track of the intermediate results of complicated calculations.

*subr (keycode 57): *Call in subroutine.* Always followed by a two-digit program-step address, *subr sends the calculator to the program subroutine that commences at that program location.

*rtn (keycode 58): *Terminate subroutine.* At the end of a subroutine, the instruction *rtn returns the calculator to the step in the main program that follows the sequence that called in the subroutine.

A program subroutine is a sequence of program steps separate from the main body of the program. It consists of a series of steps that is to be performed again and again. Written once as a subroutine, it can be called in as often as needed. Each time the calculator finishes running a subroutine, it goes back to the place in the main program where it left off, and continues from there.

A subroutine can call in sub-subroutines, which can call in sub-sub-subroutines—to four levels.

Two of the SR-56 rally scoring programs use one subroutine, and two use two subroutines. When you see how these programs work, you will appreciate the conveniences and economies that subroutines offer the SR-56 programmer.

÷ (keycode 54): *Divide*.

*Pause (keycode 59): *Pause*. As a program instruction, *pause displays for about half a second the value then in the display register; program processing then resumes.

During program execution, pressing the pause key will cause the result of each program step to be displayed for about a quarter of a second.

7 (keycode 07)

8 (keycode 08)

9 (keycode 09)

× (keycode 64): *Times, or multiply*.

*π (keycode 69): *Pi*. Enters π to twelve significant digits, displaying the value rounded to ten significant digits.

4 (keycode 04)

5 (keycode 05)

6 (keycode 06)

− (keycode 74): *Subtract*.

1 (keycode 01)

2 (keycode 02)

3 (keycode 03)

+ (keycode 84): *Add*.

0 (keycode 00)

• (keycode 92): *Decimal point.* Enter a decimal point. Pressing the key a second time during the same number entry will have no further effect; only the first point is accepted.

It is not necessary to key in the decimal point following a whole number; the calculator will place the point as soon as a function key is pressed.

+ / − (keycode 93): *Change sign.* Changes the sign of the number in the display from plus to minus or from minus to plus. (This key does not effect addition or subtraction, nor do the + and − keys perform the sign-changing function.)

= (keycode 94): *Equals.* Completes arithmetical operations and displays the answer.

There is a little more to the *equals* function than is evident at first. In subroutines, for example, if some operations in the main program are pending, = will complete *all* operations, perhaps against your wishes; this problem can be avoided by the judicious use of parentheses.

In expressions where several levels of parentheses are used, = will complete the pending operations, effectively supplying as many closing parentheses as are needed to finish off the expression. Example:

$$\frac{(9 \times 8) + (7 \times 6)}{(5 \times 4) - (3 \times 2)} = ?$$

can be solved in either of these ways:

((9 × 8) + (7 × 6)) ÷ ((5 × 4) − (3 × 2)) =
((9 × 8) + (7 × 6)) ÷ ((5 × 4) − (3 × 2 =

The ten auxiliary functions in rows 7, 8 and 9 of the keyboard need not concern us. The six that are printed in blue are statistical or engineering functions; *RAD is used in trigonometry; prt, pap and list are employed only in connection with an accessory desk printing unit that is available for use with the SR-56.

The Switches

The SR-56 has only two switches, and only one of them concerns us rallyists. Just below the display window, at the left, is a slide switch with two positions, G and D, which do not stand for an exclamation frequently heard in the heat of competition. The G means "grads," and D, "degrees." This switch is used only to select calculator modes for handling computations dealing with angles. Leave it in either position and forget it until the need for it arises. As far as rallying is concerned that will be never.

The other switch is the on/off switch. Slide it to the right, toward ON, and the display will present a zero, signifying that the calculator is ready to go to work. After the calculator has been switched on and used, switching it off kills *everything*:

The display goes blank.

The contents of the ten memory registers, the hundred program registers, the T-register and the internal processing registers are all lost.

The program counter, the subroutine-level counter and the parentheses-level counter go to sleep and will awaken only to hold zeros.

The display will wake up in floating-point mode.

The SR-56 will run on its own battery-supplied current or on power furnished through its 115-volt AC adapter/charger (included in the kit). (If the adapter/charger is connected, the battery pack *must* be in place; otherwise the calculator may be damaged.) The battery pack cannot be overcharged.

In normal use the fully charged battery pack will operate the calculator for three to six hours. The adapter/charger will recharge the pack in about four hours with the calculator switched off, about ten hours if it is switched on. It is advisable to switch the calculator off when connecting and disconnecting the adapter/charger.

The problem of keeping the calculator continuously powered for long periods in an automobile has two solutions. One is to buy one or more extra battery packs and bring them, fully charged, on the rally. These extra packs can be charged in the calculator or, with recharging equipment available from Texas Instruments, outside the calculator. (Changing battery packs kills the contents of all the SR-56's storage registers, and so should be undertaken at a checkpoint or lunch stop.) The other solution is to buy a 12VDC – 110VAC inverter of the kind designed to run an electric shaver in a car. It plugs into the cigarette lighter socket; the adapter/charger is plugged into the inverter; finally, the calculator is connected to the adapter/charger.

TI produces a 12VDC auto/boat/plane recharger for its magnetic-card programmed SR-52 pocket calculator. It is not unlikely that the company will develop a similar type for the SR-56. If you own or contemplate buying an SR-56, check with TI or your local dealer who handles the line.

The Display

The "bottom line" of the SR-56, where the answer comes out, is at the very top. In conventional notation the display shows up to ten digits. Numbers are entered into the display from right to left. The minus sign, which designates that the value displayed is negative, is always at the extreme left.

A flashing display tells you that you have made an error. You may possibly have exceeded the capacity of the calculator, or tried to calculate a root, a power or a logarithm of a negative number, or tried to divide a number by zero; or you may have tried to use more than nine levels of parentheses, or tried to stack up more than seven pending arithmetical operations. All these offenses are explained in more detail in the Owner's Manual. More likely, however, you have inadvertently pressed, manually or in a program, two arithmetical operator keys in succession without keying in an operand; for example +) or × = . Or you may have used an illegitimate program code, such as GTO 0 instead of GTO 00, having overlooked that the ten memories are numbered in single digits, 0 − 9, while the hundred program-step registers are numbered in double digits, 00 − 99.

During program execution the display goes blank except for two minus signs, which wink encouragingly until the answer—or a flashing error indication—emerges.

The Registers

Residing within the SR-56's maze of electronic circuits are 112 storage registers. These are in addition to the various processing registers, with which we are unconcerned, as they work automatically. The ones we must understand if we are to make full use of them are: the one x-register, the ten memories, the hundred program-step registers and the T-register. Let's examine them in that order.

x-register (R_x)

The x-register is also called the display register, because its content, x, is always the number that appears in the lighted display.

That is a general statement, and it needs to be qualified slightly. The display provides only ten digits, but R_x holds thirteen digits; furthermore, you can control the number of decimal places to be displayed (none to nine), thereby rounding the display. In performing calculations, however, the SR-56 always uses the full value of x to all thirteen significant digits. Check it out for yourself:

Press *fix 0 (remember that * stands for the 2nd-function key, the first key in the top row) .4999999999 × 1 =. Because you have rounded the display to zero decimal places, x appears to be 0. But now press × 2 = *fix 9, and you will see that the full value of the original x was preserved; the answer is .9999999998. Pressing *fix 0 again will give you the rounded value of the new x: 1.

Memory registers ($R_0 - R_9$)

The SR-56's ten memory registers (sometimes called storage registers, data registers or just plain memories) enable you to store and retrieve numbers—either keyboard entries or intermediate results of calculations. You park these values when it suits you to do so, and you call them back into the x-register when you need them. You can do arithmetic in the memories. And you can swap the content of any memory for the content of the x-register. The ten memories are numbered 0 − 9 and are designated as R_0, R_1, etc.

To store the value displayed in the x-register, press STO n (n being the single-digit address of the selected memory). This operation places x in R_n, overwriting the previous content of R_n.

To retrieve the value resting in R_n, press RCL n. The value is copied into R_x and is displayed, but it remains stored in R_n just in case you want to retrieve it another time.

Pressing SUM n adds the x-value to the value stored in R_n; INV SUM n subtracts x from R_n. Pressing *PROD n multiplies the value in R_n by x; INV *PROD n divides the value in R_n by x.

Pressing *EXC n places the value in R_n in R_x, simultaneously placing x in R_n.

Program registers ($R_{00} - R_{99}$)

The one hundred program registers (or program locations or program-step registers) compose the collective program memory, which is a series of keystroke instructions stored so as to constitute a calculator program. (Note that the program registers are always designated by two digits; this convention serves to distinguish proram locations 00 − 09 from memory registers 0 − 9.) Once a program has been stored it can be run automatically over and over again, and with new variables if desired.

A program remains stored until *CP is pressed (in calculate mode) or until the calculator is turned off.

T-register (R_t)

A special-purpose storage facility that is independent of all the other registers, the T-register is reachable only through the $x \leq t$ exchange key (keycode 32). We will concern ourselves not with R_t's function in polar/rectangular coordinate conversions, but with the part it plays in the tests that govern conditional program branching.

Briefly, you store in R_t the value (which may be zero) against which you wish to compare x in order to determine the one of two possible ways the program will branch. There are four comparisons: *$x = t$ (is x equal to t?); INV *$x = t$ (is x unequal to t?); *$x \geq t$ (is x equal to or greater than t?); INV *$x \geq t$ (is x less than t?). As we shall see in the chapter on SR-56 programming, if the answer to the question is yes, the calculator automatically follows one branch of the program, if the answer is no, it goes the other way.

The content of R_t is normally zero, but you may place in it any other value you choose. If you want to cause a program to branch according to whether x is a negative value, and if you know that t contains a zero, you will handle the test by storing in program memory the instruction INV *$x \geq t$. It asks, "Is x less than 0 and therefore a negative value?"

If on the other hand you want to compare x with some number other than zero, you place that number in R_t by keying it into R_x and pressing $x \leq t$; then you place x in R_x; and finally you cause the comparison to be made. If R_t is then to be cleared, the program instruction is *CP.

* * *

Although the T-register's main purpose is to implement the comparison of two values in order to determine how a program will be branched, R_t can be made to serve as a memory of a sort—in a pinch. The SR-56 Owner's Manual is silent on this usage and for several reasons we recommend it only in an emergency where no regular memory is available. One reason is that it is all too easy to inadvertently leave a no longer wanted value in R_t. Another is the difficulty of clearing R_t when the calculator is in calculate mode. You can key in $0 x \leq t$, to be sure, but there you lose the current x. In calculate mode, pressing *CP clears R_t—but if a program is stored, it clears the program memory as well. On principle, use R_t as a working memory only when $R_0 - R_9$ are all full, and then only with due caution.

Calculating With The SR-56

Run-of-the-mill calculations with an algebraic-notation calculator like the SR-56 are quite simple:

12 + 34 = ?

Keystrokes: 1 2 + 3 4 = (answer: 46.)

98 − 76 = ?

Keystrokes: 9 8 − 7 6 = (answer: 22.)

45 × 5.6 =?

Keystrokes: 4 5 × 5 . 6 = (answer: 252.)

0.45 ÷ 5.6 =?

Keystrokes: . 4 5 ÷ 5 . 6 = (answer: .0803571429)

Chain calculations can be somewhat more involved:

$$\frac{(12 + 34) \times (98 - 76)}{(45 \div 56)} = ?$$

Key	Display	Key	Display	Key	Display
(	0.	(	46.	(	1012.
1	1	9	9	4	4
2	12	8	98	5	45
+	12.	−	98.	÷	45.
3	3	7	7	5	5
4	34	6	76	6	56
)	46.	)	22.	)	.8035714286
×	46.	÷	1012.	=	1259.3777

Note that a very slightly different equation is handled considerably differently:

$$\frac{(12 + 34) + (98 - 76)}{(45 \div 56)} = ?$$

Key	Display	Key	Display	Key	Display
(	0.	(	46.	(	68.
(	0.	9	9	4	4
1	1	8	98	5	45
2	12	−	98.	÷	45.
+	12.	7	7	5	5
3	3	6	76	6	56
4	34	)	22.	)	.80357...
)	46.	)	68.	=	84.622222
+	46.	÷	68.		

Although there is nothing essentially difficult about algebraic notation, the SR-56's rather sophisticated use of algebraic hierarchy—the sequence in which it handles pending arithmetical operations—deserves study. It gives the calculator a vast amount of power, and needs to be understood if full advantage is to be taken of that power. Read all about it in the Owner's Manual.

Chapter 9
Navigational Arithmetic

THIS BOOK assumes that you are conversant with rally math and are looking for a better way to solve the average-speed problem. Whatever you have been using—pencil and paper, tables, Curta—the SR-56 will do the job easier and faster. Let's review the basics and see how the SR-56 handles them.

The Time-Speed-Distance Equation

The equation $D = R \times T$ (*distance* equals *rate* multiplied by *time*) and its corollaries $R = D \div T$ and $T = D \div R$ are the key to all the variations on the average-speed theme. Here are the equations expressed in the commonly used units:

$$miles = mph \times hours \qquad miles = \frac{mph \times minutes}{60}$$

$$miles = \frac{mph \times seconds}{3600}$$

$$mph = \frac{miles}{hours} \qquad mph = \frac{miles \times 60}{minutes}$$

$$mph = \frac{miles \times 3600}{seconds}$$

$$hours = \frac{miles}{mph} \qquad minutes = \frac{miles \times 60}{mph}$$

$$seconds = \frac{miles \times 3600}{mph}$$

If you have an SR-56, work out the following problems for practice; if not, these examples will show you how the SR-56 solves them.

(a) You are to drive for 12 minutes at 37.5 mph; what distance will you cover?

$$D = \frac{37.5 \times 12}{60}$$

Switch on the power and press 37.5 × 12 ÷ 60 =. The answer displayed is 7.5 (miles).

Note that you could press 37.5 × 12 = ÷ 60 =, or (37.5 × 12) ÷ 60 =; sometimes, if you are concerned with observing intermediate answers, such a method is worth the few extra keystrokes.

(b) You have 16 minutes to drive 9 miles; what average speed must you maintain?

$$R = \frac{9 \times 60}{16}$$

Press 9 × 60 ÷ 16 =; the instant answer is 33.75 (mph).

(c) You are to drive 11.23 miles at an average speed of 29.65 mph; how long will it take?

$$T = \frac{11.23}{29.65}$$

Press 11.23 ÷ 29.65 =; the answer is .3787521079 (hour). How many minutes is that? Press × 60 = and see: 22.72512648 minutes. You can settle for 22.73 minutes if you like (*fix 2 will give you that). If you want the decimal part of the minute in seconds press INV *Int × 60 = and you will have it: 43.51 seconds. The answer, then, is 22 minutes 43.51 seconds.

The Odometer Check

You may not remember, but as late as the early 1950s, when the odometer check was waiting to be invented, you had a considerable advantage, other things begin equal (as they usually were), if you happened to be rallying in a car identical to the rallymaster's. Intolerable? Not at all! Timing was to the nearest minute, and the dollar alarm clocks at some checkpoints didn't even have a second hand.

---
*Denotes 2nd function key.

Nowadays all average-speed rallies start with a measured run of several miles that enables you to compare your odometer with the official instrument. If yours does not match the official one exactly, you (or your calculator) must adjust your calculated allowed driving times by the percentage of difference. Otherwise, if your odometer reads higher than the official mileage, you will tend to run late; if it reads lower, you will tend to run early. Mnemonically, *l*ong = *l*ate, and *s*hort = *t*oo *s*oon. Moreover, if the rally directions require you to do something at a place so many official miles beyond some other place, you have to apply the same percentage of difference (just about universally called "error," although it is nothing of the kind) to the official mileage in order to determine where the place will be according to your odometer.

The Correction Factors

Two correction factors, in this book called Factor A and Factor B, have to be calculated at the end of the odometer check.

$$\text{Factor A} = \frac{\text{official distance}}{\text{odometer distance}} \qquad \text{Factor B} = \frac{\text{odometer distance}}{\text{official distance}}$$

The factors have several uses:

official distance = odometer distance × Factor A

odometer distance = official distance × Factor B

indicated (corrected) speed = official speed × Factor B

indicated (corrected) minutes per mile = official minutes per mile × Factor A

Assume that at the end of an odometer check of 20.05 official miles your odometer reads 19.97 miles. Then Factor A is 20.05 ÷ 19.97 = 1.004006009.

To get Factor B you need not key in 19.97 ÷ 20.05 =. With Factor A still displayed, just press *1/*x* and you have it: .9960099751. When the two factors are stored in memories, they can be drawn on as often as needed to adjust the answers to navigational problems by the complement, speaking very strictly, of the percentage of difference between your odometer and the official one. (It shouldn't be necessary, but we'll remind you anyway that "no odometer differ-

---
*Denotes 2nd function key.

ence" does not mean factors of 0. If at the end of a check of 10.00 miles your odometer reads 10.00 miles, you must still divide the official distance by the indicated distance and store both Factor A and Factor B as 1. The reason is that if you ask the calculator to multiply your uncorrected allowed time by 0, then 0 is what you'll get for the answer.)

Quite possibly you are reflecting that Factor B is not really necessary—that since it is the reciprocal of Factor A (1 ÷ Factor A), multiplying official distance by Factor B is exactly the same as dividing it by Factor A. You are indisputably right. We can offer no compelling reason for suggesting two factors except that it seemed a good idea, conceptually, at the time we were developing the navigational programs. The point is scarcely worth arguing; let it stand as testimony to the fact that in calculator programming, as in many of life's other endeavors, there is no one way, or even one best way, and any way that works is a good way.

Special Problems

Even though you may have a program stored in the calculator and ready to run whenever you wish, the calculator's computing functions are still available—except while the program is actually running—for performing manual computations. The only proviso is that the side calculations you do manually must not disturb the contents of any memory that the program will call upon. Thus the SR-56 can always serve to solve the ancillary navigational challenges that are always being thrown in by imaginative rallymasters for your delectation. We can't cover them all here—many haven't even been thought of yet—but we can analyze some representative types and perhaps put you in a frame of mind to deal with others.

The Average of the Averages

"Drive the first half of the next leg at 30 mph, and the second half at 45 mph."

Since you don't know how long the leg is, what you have to find out is the average of the two average speeds. No, you cannot add 30 and 45 and divide by 2 and drive at 37 1/2 mph. The reason is that as you will be driving a longer time at 30 than you will drive at 45, your average speed will be less than the arithmetic mean. What you are after is the *harmonic* mean:

$$\frac{2}{\frac{1}{30} + \frac{1}{45}}$$

If you prefer it another way, it's twice the product of the two speeds divided by their sum:

$$\frac{2 \times (30 \times 45)}{30 + 45}$$

There are several ways to set up this expression for the SR-56. One, and possibly the safest, as it posits all the parentheses imaginably necessary, is this:

$$2 \div ((1 \div 30) + (1 \div 45)) =$$

More simply:

$$2 \div (1 \div 30 + 1 \div 45 =$$

Still another way, rather more sophisticated:

$$2 \div (30 \ *1/x + 45 \ */x =$$

All give the same answer: 36 mph.

If you were told to drive at an average speed that would be equivalent to your driving the first third of a leg at 20 mph, the second third at 25 mph, and the last third at 30 mph, the formula would be:

$$\frac{3}{1/20 + 1/25 + 1/30}$$

The keystrokes: $3 \div (1 \div 20 + 1 \div 25 + 1 \div 30 =$. The answer: 24.32432432 mph.

Percentages

It would probably be difficult today to catch a rallyist out with an instruction like this:

> Your average speed is 28 mph. At Point A decrease your average speed by 5 percent. At Point B increase your average speed by 5 percent.

We mention it here only to note that the SR-56's lack of a percent key is no disadvantage. Here's the drill:

$$28 - CE \times .05 =$$

That gives you 26.6 mph. Now, with that answer still displayed:

+ CE × .05 =

And your third speed is 27.93 mph.

You could as easily have pressed 28 − 28 × .05 = + 26.6 × .05 =. But here CE has the effect of repeating the displayed number, saving you a few keystrokes.

There is of course another way: 28 × .95 = × 1.05 = .

"Phantom Car" Problems

Navigational puzzles involving the antics of imaginary vehicles can be dreamed up in virtually infinite variety. Although their arithmetic is seldom difficult, analyzing such a problem and setting it up for solution can strain a navigator's composure, especially where he has to watch a tricky route and simultaneously anticipate an early action point. Sometimes panic is hard to avoid, but taking a methodical approach always helps. Contemplate this nauseous supplementary instruction, handed to you as you are timed in at a control:

> Your average speed is 36 mph. Exactly 5 minutes before you are due to leave this checkpoint, a man on a phantom bicycle takes off from right beside you and precedes you along the rally route at 9 mph.
>
> At the exact moment you start the leg, a phantom car starts driving toward you and the cyclist, from a point 5 1/2 miles farther along on the rally route, at a constant speed. Exactly 3 minutes 20 seconds after overtaking the bicycle you meet the phantom car. At this point change your average speed to that of the phantom car.

Go after the unknowns in the order in which you may reasonably expect to find them. First off, how long and how far is it to the place where you catch up with the cyclist? It helps to remember that $D = R \times T$ and to reflect that if it takes you x minutes to catch the nimble bicycle, the cyclist will have been pedaling for $x + 5$ minutes, and that you and he will have covered the same distance. Then $36x = 9(x + 5)$; $36x = 9x + 45$; $27x = 45$; $x = 1.667$ minutes, or 1 min. 40 sec. How far? Again $D = R \times T$, and $D = (36 \times 1.667) \div 60 = 1$ mile. The man on the bicycle may have had a 5-minute head start, but your speed was four times his.

At that same speed, 36 mph, you press on for another 3 minutes 20 seconds, or 3.333 minutes. D is *still* equal to $R \times T$, and so the next little hop measures out at (36 × 3.333) ÷ 60 = 2 miles. So you meet the phantom car 1 + 2 = 3 miles from the start of the leg.

You have now been driving 1.667 + 3.333 = 5 minutes—and so has the phantom car, which in that time has covered 5.5 − 3 = 2.5 miles. Its speed (and your next speed) is what? Since $R = D \div T = (2.5 \times 60) \div 5$, the answer is 30 mph. And there you are—except for one more thing. *Where* do you change speed to 30? After 3 miles, yes, but bear in mind that that's 3 *official* miles. By your odometer it's 3 × Factor B.

In their less complex forms, most phantom-car problems are amenable to solution by one or another of eighteen formuals given in the Appendix. Here is an example.

> As you leave this checkpoint at 42 mph, a phantom car 10 miles farther along the route sets off on the official course, in the same direction as you, at 27 mph. Where you overtake the phantom car turn left. From the Appendix, the formula is

$$D = \frac{BC}{B - A}$$

where A = speed of phantom car in miles per hour
B = speed of rally car in miles per hour
C = miles phantom car is ahead at the start
D = miles to be driven by rally car to overtake phantom car

$A = 27$; $B = 42$; $C = 10$. Then the keystrokes are:

$$42 \times 10 \div (42 - 27 =$$

Answer: 28 miles.

Chapter 10
Programming the SR-56

IF YOU CAN solve a problem manually with the SR-56, you can program the calculator to solve the same problem, automatically, again and again, using the same or different numbers. To program the SR-56 you simply store in the program memory the same keystrokes you used to solve the program manually. Once they are stored, the calculator will perform them for you, in sequence, at the press of the R/S (run/stop) key.

As you might expect, there is a certain procedure that you must follow:

1. Solve the problem manually, making sure that the method and the answer are correct.
2. Write down the individual steps, keystroke by keystroke, in the proper sequence, numbering the first keystroke 00, the second 01, and so on. (The limit is 100 steps, the last being numbered 99.)
3. Press 2nd CP to clear the program memory. (If the calculator has just been switched on, this step is not necessary; nevertheless it's a good habit to get into.)
4. Press LRN. This puts the calculator in *learn mode*. The display will read 00 00, indicating that the calculator is ready to accept program instruction 00. As soon as you have keyed it in, the display will change to 01 00. The

program counter—the first two digits—now tells you that the calculator is ready for instruction 01. (The second pair of digits is reserved for the program keycodes, which will be displayed when you single-step through the entered program to make sure you have keyed in the program instructions correctly.)

5. When you have keyed in the last program step, press LRN again to place the calculator in *execute mode* (or *manual mode*); then press RST to set the program counter to 00.

The program is actually ready to run; however, it is always advisable to check the program codes to make sure you have not made a mistake in keying in the program. Press LRN again. The display now shows the first program step number (00), followed by the corresponding keycode. Verify the code and press SST; now displayed is 01, followed by its keycode.

Check to the end of the program. If you discover that you have made a mistake, you had best switch the calculator off and start all over again, although the Owner's Manual explains how you can rectify some program-entry errors by overwriting them.

6. When the program finally checks out to your satisfaction, press LRN RST. The program counter is now at 00 and the calculator is in execute mode, ready to run your program.

We'll review the procedure using a simple problem but one that can be varied sufficiently to demonstrate some of the ways in which programs for the SR-56 can be elaborated.

Constructing a Program

Suppose that you have several Centigrade temperatures to convert to Fahrenheit. You know the general formula, of course:

$$°F = (°C \times 1.8) + 32$$

The temperatures to be converted are 100°C, 37°C, 0°C and −40°C. You can switch on your SR-56 and do the job this way:

Keystrokes	Display
100 × 1.8 + 32 =	212.
37 × 1.8 + 32 =	98.6
0 × 1.4 + 32 =	32.
40 +/− × 1.8 + 32 =	− 40.

You have obtained your four answers without undue strain. Still, you have had to press the keys ×1.8 + 32 = four times. If you had many more temperatures to convert, you might well get tired of repeating those same eight keystrokes time after time. What you need is a program that, after you have keyed in just the temperature to be converted, will automatically press the rest of the keys for you.

You know how to solve the equation manually; therefore you know how to write the steps into program form. Switch the calculator on and press these keys:

Keystrokes	Display	Comment
LRN	00 00	Calculator is in learn mode; program counter is at 00; calculator is ready for you to key in instruction 00
×	01 00	Program counter (first two digits) always shows the number of the *next* program step to be entered
1	02 00	Ready for step 02
.	03 00	Ready for step 03 . . .
8	04 00	
+	05 00	
3	06 00	
2	07 00	
=	08 00	
R/S	09 00	
RST	10 00	Ready for step 10. But there is no step 10. So:
LRN	0	Calculator is now in execute-program (or calculate) mode

To make certain that you have entered the program correctly, it is *always* advisable to verify the keycodes. The check takes only a minute or so, and it will uncover any keying error you may have made, such as failing to press a button, pressing the wrong button or inadvertently pressing the same button more than once.

To check the keycodes, refer to the charts on pages 105 and 106 (they will serve until you have memorized the codes) and press these keys:

Keystrokes	Display	Keystrokes	Display
RST	0	SST	06 02
LRN	00 64	SST	07 94
SST	01 01	SST	08 41
SST	02 92	SST	09 42
SST	03 08	LRN	0
SST	04 84	RST	0
SST	05 03		

What if the check does reveal an error? Suppose that while single-stepping through this program you find that you accidentally pressed the 9 instead of the 8 at step 03; the keycode display reads 03 09. Simply press 8. Then you can press *bst to confirm the correction. The display now should show 03 08.

The last two keystrokes, LRN and RST, have restored the execute mode and set the program counter to step 00. You are ready to make your four conversions automatically. Press 100 R/S; the answer should be displayed as 212. Then 37 R/S should give 98.6; 0 R/S should give 32.; and 40 +/− R/S should give − 40.

Perfecting a Program

So well has your program dealt with the boiling point of water, the normal oral temperature of a healthy human, the freezing point of water (at sea level, of course!) and the one instance where Fahrenheit and Celsius notations converge that you decide to make a whole series of similar conversions and find all the Fahrenheit equivalents of the Centigrade temperatures from 0° to 100° at 5-degree intervals. But you suspect that you can do better than sit and key in 0 R/S, 5 R/S . . . 100 R/S. Indeed you can. What you want to do is to start with 0 and then add 5 every time a conversion has been made. No problem. Place the calculator in learn mode (press RST LRN) and enter this program:

LOC	CODE	KEY	LOC	CODE	KEY	LOC	CODE	KEY	LOC	CODE	KEY
00	33	STO	05	01	1	10	02	2	15	00	0
01	00	0	06	92	.	11	94	=	16	22	GTO
02	34	RCL	07	08	8	12	59	*pause	17	00	0
03	00	0	08	84	+	13	05	5	18	02	2
04	64	×	09	03	3	14	35	SUM			

*Denotes 2nd function key

Press LRN RST 0 R/S—and the answers will appear at the rate of about one a second—so quickly, in fact, that you soon lost track of the Centigrade temperature being converted. That problem is easily remedied with a simple pause instruction at the fifth step. Of course you have to reenter most of the program, but that is the price of progress. Here is the new routine:

LOC	CODE	KEY	LOC	CODE	KEY	LOC	CODE	KEY
00	33	STO	07	92	.	14	05	5
01	00	0	08	08	8	15	35	SUM
02	34	RCL	09	84	+	16	00	0
03	00	0	10	03	3	17	22	GTO
04	59	*pause	11	02	2	18	00	0
05	64	×	12	94	=	19	02	2
06	01	1	13	59	*pause			

Having stored this program, press LRN RST 0 R/S. The display presents the first C temperature, 0, followed by its F equivalent, 32. Then come 5, 41; 10, 50; 15, 59; and so on until 100, 212, where you press R/S (sometimes you have to press R/S and hold it down for an instant) to end program execution.

Jolly good! But why not make the calculator halt itself? You can manage it easily enough by adding to the program a conditional test and a program branch. You will order the calculator to ascertain whether the last C temperature converted was 100 degrees. If so, the calculator is to branch to a series of steps that will halt program execution. If not, it is to make another conversion, follow with another test, and so proceed until the predetermined limit of 100 is reached. This modified program does exactly that:

LOC	CODE	KEY	LOC	CODE	KEY	LOC	CODE	KEY
00	33	STO	10	03	3	21	02	2
01	00	0	11	02	2	22	09	9
02	34	RCL	12	94	=	23	05	5
03	00	0	13	59	*pause	24	35	SUM
04	59	*pause	14	01	1	25	00	0
05	64	×	15	00	0	26	22	GTO
06	01	1	16	00	0	27	00	0
07	92	.	17	32	$x \leq t$	28	02	2
08	08	8	18	34	RCL	29	41	R/S
09	84	+	20	37	*$x = t$	30	42	RST

*Denotes 2nd function key

After you have stored the program, be sure to press LRN. Then press RST 0 R/S. The calculator makes the conversions up to including 100°C = 212°F and stops, all as ordered.

After each conversion has been made and displayed, steps 14 – 17 place the limit, 100, in R_t. Steps 18 – 19 recall the last C temperature. Step 20 asks whether that temperature (x) equals the limit 100 (t). Watch what happens when the test is made: If the answer is yes, the calculator moves to steps 21 – 22, which send it on to steps 29 – 30, which halt the program. If the answer is no, the calculator automatically skips the two instructions that immediately follow the test, moving to step 23. Steps 23 – 25 add 5 to the last C temperature, which is in R_0. Steps 26 – 28 send the calculator back to step 02, where it starts another conversion.

Although the program works well enough, a little reflection turns up some faults. For one thing, it is wasteful; there is really no need to place 100 in R_t every time the program runs. Furthermore, suppose that you wanted to use an increment of 10 degrees rather than 5; that would mean rewriting the program from step 23 onward so as to make room for the second digit—and steps 21 – 22 would have to be amended to contain the address 30.

With nine memories unused, we ought to be able to improve the program by stashing some of the parameters in idle storage registers, thereby gaining both convenience and flexibility. Let's use R_0 for the beginning C temperature, R_1 for the limit, and R_2 for the increment. The memories will hold as many digits as the calculator will accept, and will place them in R_x promptly on request.

At the same time let's give some thought to the conditional test. It serves all right for a starting temperature of 0, an increment of 5 and a limit of 100. But what if you wanted (a) to start with 0, (b) to use an increment of 3 and (c) to halt the conversions when the newly incremented temperature reached or exceeded 100? It is quite clear that the incremented temperature will never be exactly 100; it will go 0, 3 . . . 99, 102. Consequently, the conditional test $x = t$ where $t = 100$ can never be answered affirmatively, and the calculator will persist until things grow very warm indeed!

The test will have to be changed to *$x \geq t$: "Is x equal to or greater than t?" Additional thought on the sequence of operations discovers the advisability of depositing the temperature limit in R_t

---

*Denotes 2nd function key

early in the game—and only once. And so the refining process brings us to this:

LOC	CODE	KEY	LOC	CODE	KEY	LOC	CODE	KEY
00	34	RCL	10	84	+	20	34	RCL
01	01	1	11	03	3	21	02	2
02	32	$x \leq t$	12	02	2	22	35	SUM
03	34	RCL	13	94	=	23	00	0
04	00	0	14	59	*pause	24	22	GTO
05	59	*pause	15	34	RCL	25	00	0
06	64	×	16	00	0	26	03	3
07	01	1	17	47	*$x \geq t$	27	41	R/S
08	92	.	18	02	2	28	42	RST
09	08	8	19	07	7			

Press LRN and store the three parameters:

Starting temperature	0 STO 0
Temperature limit	100 STO 1
Temperature increment	3 STO 2

Press RST R/S. The conversion will start with 0/32 and continue until 102/215.6 has been displayed. Then, the limit of 100 having been exceeded, calculations will stop.

Now consider a rather subtle point. If you had some reason for not going beyond the 100-degree limit—in other words, if you wanted to stop at 99 and not go so far as 102—you would have to modify the conditional test and perform it earlier in the program. You might then come up with something like this:

LOC	CODE	KEY	LOC	CODE	KEY	LOC	CODE	KEY
00	34	RCL	09	32	$x \leq t$	19	59	*pause
01	00	0	10	59	*pause	20	34	RCL
02	32	$x \leq t$	11	64	×	21	02	2
			12	01	1	22	35	SUM
03	34	RCL	13	92	.	23	00	0
04	01	1	14	08	8	24	42	RST
05	12	INV	15	84	+	25	15	CLR
06	47	*$x \geq t$	16	03	3	26	41	R/S
07	02	2	17	02	2	27	42	RST
08	05	5	18	94	=			

*Denotes 2nd function key

The three parameters are stored as before. Press RST R/S.

Steps 00 – 02 call in the starting temperature from R_0 and place it in R_t. Steps 03 – 04 place in R_x the limit stored in R_1. Steps 05 – 06 ask: "Is the limit x less than the temperature t that is being tested?" In other words, does the most recently incremented temperature exceed the limit?

If the answer is yes, it's time to quit; steps 07 – 08 send the calculator to steps 25 – 27, which clear the display and halt program execution.

If the answer is no (meaning that we're not at the limit yet), the calculator skips to step 09, which recalls from R_t the temperature to be converted. Step 10 displays that value, and steps 11 – 19 effect the conversion and display the °F answer. Steps 20 – 23 increment the value in R_0, and step 24 sends the calculator back to step 00 to begin a new program run.

Time-Conversion Routines

That, you say, is all very well, but what does it have to do with rallying? The answer of course is nothing, but these variations of a basic program do serve to illustrate some valuable principles. There is more that you should know, however, and so let's turn to a program that does have something to do with rallying.

Like every other rallyist, you know the difficulties that arise whenever you have to add or subtract times that are expressed in hours, minutes and seconds. Say you left a checkpoint at 10:37:47 and finished the leg at 11:02:03. What was your elapsed time? There is no way to subtract the earlier time from the later time directly, either on paper or with the SR-56.* About the best you can do on paper is to write:

$$11:02:03 = 11:01:63 = 10:61:63$$
$$- 10:37:47$$
$$= 00:24:16$$

Ironically, it is easier to work it out on paper than to try to perform the calculations manually using the SR-56. A great many hand calculations, though, can be quite a chore. What if you were

---

*The Hewlett-Packard HP-25 (and HP-25C) and the Texas Instruments magnetic-card-programmed SR-52 do provide automatic conversion between hours-minutes-seconds times and decimal-hours times.

scoring a hundred-car rally that had ten checkpoints? Doesn't the SR-56 offer a better way? Indeed it does, if the number of calculations to be performed justifies entering a rather long program.

The objective of the program we are going to develop is, you of course understand, to change the conventionally expressed time notation—hours, minutes, seconds—to a single unit; we are, in a word, homogenizing. One approach would be to reduce everything to seconds:

$$\begin{array}{rl} 11 \text{ hours} \times 3600 = & 39{,}600 \text{ seconds} \\ 2 \text{ minutes} \times 60 = & 120 \text{ seconds} \\ 3 \text{ seconds} = & \underline{3 \text{ seconds}} \\ \text{adding:} & 39{,}723 \text{ seconds} \end{array}$$

Taking the 11, and 2 and the 3 as separate integers, the calculator routine is easy enough:

$$(11 \times 3600) + (2 \times 60) + 3 =$$

And as it happens, you can even omit the parentheses.

But if you intend to key in the hours-minutes-seconds time as a single value like 11.0203—where the point is not a decimal but a separator—the procedure gets more complicated:

(11.0203 STO 0 *Int × 3600) + (RCL 0 INV *Int × 100) STO 0 *Int × 60) + (RCL 0 INV *Int × 100 =

This is the only way out, though, unless you are prepared to store the 11 in one memory, the 2 in another, and the 3 in still another. The trouble with that is that the number of memories is limited, and as a matter of principle, calculator programs (to say nothing of computer programs) should be as economical as possible of storage facilities as well as program steps.

The road back—reconverting, that is, from 39,723 seconds to 11.0203—is rather more involved. (You might find it rewarding, even entertaining, to work it out for yourself.)

Empirical methodology (translation: plain old trial and error) reveals that it is somewhat easier to convert hours, minutes and seconds to minutes and decimal minutes; indeed, the rally scoring programs you will encounter later on do exactly that. For our object-lesson right now, however, let's decide to convert to hours and decimal hours. Then the routine goes like this:

(11.0203 STO 0 *Int) + (RCL 0 INV *Int × 100) STO 0 *Int ÷ 60) + (RCL 0 INV *Int ÷ 36 =

---
*Denotes 2nd function key

The answer comes up 11.03416667 hours, or if you want to press *fix 4, 11.0342 hours: 11 and 342/10,000 hours, that is.

The return trip too is lengthy, but it takes you back to 11.0203: (11.0342 STO 0 *Int) + (RCL 0 INV *Int × 60) STO 0 *Int ÷ 100) + (RCL 0 INV *Int × .006 =

A dual program, about half of it (steps 00 – 31) devoted to converting hours, minutes and seconds to decimal hours, the rest (steps 32 – 65) to converting decimal hours to hours, minutes and seconds, is now easy to construct:

LOC	CODE	KEY	LOC	CODE	KEY	LOC	CODE	KEY
00	33	STO	22	34	RCL	44	53	)
01	00	0	23	00	0	45	33	STO
02	29	*Int	24	12	INV	46	00	0
03	84	+	25	29	*Int	47	29	*Int
04	52	(	26	54	÷	48	54	÷
05	34	RCL	27	03	3	49	01	1
06	00	0	28	06	6	50	00	0
07	12	INV	29	94	=	51	00	0
08	29	*Int	30	41	R/S	52	53	)
09	64	×	31	42	RST	53	84	+
10	01	1	32	33	STO	54	34	RCL
11	00	0	33	00	0	55	00	0
12	00	0	34	29	*Int	56	12	INV
13	53	)	35	84	+	57	29	*Int
14	33	STO	36	52	(	58	64	×
15	00	0	37	34	RCL	59	92	•
16	29	*Int	38	00	0	60	00	0
17	54	÷	39	12	INV	61	00	0
18	06	6	40	29	*Int	62	06	6
19	00	0	41	64	×	63	94	=
20	53	)	42	06	6	64	41	R/S
21	84	+	43	00	0	65	42	RST

Load the program, return to execute mode and press *fix 4 to limit the display to four places. Now key in 11.0203 (for 11 hrs. 2 min. 3 sec.) and press RST R/S. When the answer, 11.0342 hours, comes up, the calculator stops at step 30. To convert another

---

*Denotes 2nd function key

hours-minutes-seconds time, merely key it in and press R/S. If you want to change 11.0342 back to hours, minutes and seconds, key it in if it is not still in R_x, then press GTO 32 R/S.

The truncation process is much used here (steps 02, 08 − 09, 16, 24 − 25, 34, 39 − 40, 47, 56 − 57); in fact, if it were not possible to deal separately with the integer and the fraction of a decimal number, it would be rather awkward for a hand calculator to accomplish these conversions. It could be done, but hardly economically, as three memories would be needed. Here only one memory is used.

Subroutines

A useful feature of the SR-56 is its provision for program subroutines. Where the same string of instructions occurs several times in a program, that series can be written once, separate from the main part of the program, and called in whenever it is needed. The effect is to send the calculator from the main program to the subroutine, execute the subroutine and return the calculator to the place in the program where it left off.

The command to call a subroutine is *subr *nn*—*nn* being the two-digit program location where the subroutine starts. The last step in a subroutine must always be *rtn.

For an example of how a subroutine is utilized, look back at the sixty-six-step time-converting program we've been discussing. You will see three strings of repeated instructions: 00 − 09/32 − 41, 13 − 17/44 − 48 and 20 − 25/52 − 57. Clearly, there are possibilities for subroutines here. But let's not go overboard, because although subroutines do save program steps, not every opportunity proves to be economical. It takes three steps to call in a subroutine, and an extra step at the end of the subroutine to send the calculator back to the main program. If a subroutine is to be used only twice, then, it will not save anything unless it consists of more than eight steps. For that reason we should consider making a subroutine only of steps 00 − 09 and 32 − 41. At that, we save only three steps, but where a program threatens to exceed the hundred-step limit, every saving helps tremendously.

Here is the time-conversion program with the subroutine tacked on at steps 52 − 62. It is called in first at steps 00 − 02; step

---

*Denotes 2nd function key

62 sends the calculator back to step 03; the subroutine is called again at steps 25 – 27, and the **main program resumes at step 28.**

LOC	CODE	KEY	LOC	CODE	KEY	LOC	CODE	KEY
00	57	*subr	21	06	6	42	12	INV
01	05	5	22	94	=	43	29	*Int
02	02	2	23	41	R/S	44	64	×
03	01	1	24	42	RST	45	92	.
04	00	0	25	57	*subr	46	00	0
05	00	0	26	05	5	47	00	0
06	53	)	27	02	2	48	06	6
07	33	STO	28	06	6	49	94	=
08	00	0	29	00	0	50	41	R/S
09	29	*Int	30	53	)	51	42	RST
10	54	÷	31	33	STO	52	33	STO
11	06	6	32	00	0	53	00	0
12	00	0	33	29	*Int	54	29	*Int
13	53	)	34	54	÷	55	84	+
14	84	+	35	01	1	56	52	(
15	34	RCL	36	00	0	57	34	RCL
16	00	0	37	00	0	58	00	0
17	12	INV	38	53	)	59	12	INV
18	29	*Int	39	84	+	60	29	*Int
19	54	÷	40	34	RCL	61	64	×
20	03	3	41	00	0	62	58	*rtn

Fix four decimal places. To convert clock time to decimal hours, key in the clock time as hours, decimal point, minutes and seconds and press RST R/S. To convert decimal hours time to clock time, key in the decimal hours and press GTO 25 R/S. Clock-time answers like 3.1960, a result of rounding discrepancies, must be read as 3:20:00.

It is possible to write a subroutine to a subroutine; you will find some instances in the rally scoring programs in Chapter 14.

* * *

Needless to say, this short lesson in **SR**-56 programming tells you far less than you will want to know. It should be enough, however, to let you move along and see how the rally navigation programs work.

---
*Denotes 2nd function key

Chapter 11
SR-56 Rally
Navigation Programs

THE ELECTRONIC ROAD to average-speed navigation at once resembles and differs from the route that is so familiar to Curta users. Both methods are based on the same general equation: *time = distance ÷ speed*. Specifically, the Curta multiplied distance by a minutes-per-mile factor corrected for odometer difference, and the equation was in fact this:

$$\text{allowed time in minutes} = \text{miles} \times \frac{60 \times \text{official distance}}{\text{mph} \times \text{odometer distance}}$$

with $60 \div mph$ being the minutes-per-mile factor. The distance traveled according to the contestant's odometer was built up by cranking up a distance increment.

The programs for the electronic calculator utilize the very same equation, but in a somewhat different fashion. The Curta's multiplier was a distance increment, which was measured—counted if you will—by crank turns; its multiplicand was the minutes-per-mile factor, which you had to recalculate at every speed change and enter by positioning the slides. The electronic machine is content to recalculate the corrected factor every time you run the program, saving you the trouble of figuring it even once. But let's not get ahead of ourselves. Some thought about what we want from a calculator program will help us to decide how to write it. The system should do these things:

1. Calculate, as often as desired, the driving time—corrected for odometer difference—allowed for any distance at any average speed.
2. Display the distance to the hundredth of a mile.
3. Display the time in conformity with the competing crew's timepieces: in minutes and seconds, in minutes and hundredths (or both) or as clock time.
4. Calculate and display on demand the official-distance equivalent of the odometer distance.
5. Calculate and display on demand the odometer-distance equivalent of any official distance.
6. Handle mid-leg speed changes without requiring the navigator to do any more than key in the odometer reading at the speed-change point, run the program to update the data, and store in memory the new average speed.
7. Handle "pauses" and "gain-time" instructions by increasing or decreasing the allowed time independently of distance.
8. Readily accept adjustments necessitated by the car's straying from the rally course.
9. Display on demand, for verification or review, any current answer or stored data.
10. Permit running an entire rally with no more than one odometer or more than one timepiece, and without requiring any adjustment or resetting of either the odometer or the timepiece between scoring checkpoints.
11. Pass all these minor miracles without resort to the Curta's infamous distance increment. In other words we want to be able to key in the distance according to our odometer and produce all the answers without, as they say, further ado. And what do we propose to offer our calculator to work with? Only these: the given average speed, the official length of the odometer check, our end-of-the-check odometer reading and, periodically, the distance our odometer tells us we have driven.

Can the SR-56 manage? Indeed it can—cheerfully, reliably, precisely, virtually instantly, always tirelessly. We need only store the parameters and tell the calculator, through the program, where to find them and what to do with them.

We will, arbitrarily, store the raw data so:

> The stated average speed in R_2.
> 60 in R_3; we know that if we want the allowed time in minutes we must include this value in the numerator of the *t-s-d* equation.
> Factor A (the official length of the odometer check divided by our indicated odometer distance) in R_4.
> Factor B (the reciprocal of Factor A) in R_5.

We will, again arbitrarily, reserve other calculator memories for other purposes:

> R_0 to accumulate the allowed driving time.
> R_1 for the odometer distance.
> R_6 for the official-distance equivalent of the mileage in R_1.
> R_7, R_8 and R_9 for use in later, more elaborate programs.

To solve the average-speed equation, we need merely multiply the distance of interest by 60, divide that product by the average speed, and multiply the quotient by Factor A. Just before displaying the answer, the calculator should display the odometer distance, as a reminder and verification. Meanwhile the official-distance equivalent of that distance should be calculated and stored for retrieval when and if we need it.

The chain of simple multiply-and-divide calculations can be programmed with the greatest of ease. Suppose the average speed is 30 mph and our odometer read 9.95 at the end of the 10.00-mile odometer check. The times for the first few miles work out in this manner:

Odometer distance	Calculation	Answer
1 mile	$1 \times \dfrac{60}{30} \times \dfrac{10}{9.95} =$	2.01 minutes

Odometer distance	Calculation	Answer
2 miles	$2 \times \dfrac{60}{30} \times \dfrac{10}{9.95} =$	4.02 minutes
3 miles	$3 \times \dfrac{60}{30} \times \dfrac{10}{9.95} =$	6.03 minutes

But a speed change to 35 mph takes place at 3.75 miles:

3.75 miles	$3.75 \times \dfrac{60}{30} \times \dfrac{10}{9.95} =$	7.54 minutes

What now? We cannot, alas, substitute 35 for 30 and find the allowed time at the end of 4 miles by performing $4 \times (60 \div 35) \times (10 \div 9.95)$. We are therefore going to have to back off and look for a somewhat different approach. To define the problem, what we want is to get the correct allowed time for 4 miles by adding to 7.54 minutes the corrected allowed time for 0.25 mile at 35 mph.

Does this mean that we must resort to the Curta's distance-increment method after all? In principle, yes; in practice, no. We cannot possibly escape having to accumulate the allowed running time as the total of times allowed for a number of incremental distances. But instead of having to select a regular increment (like 1 mile or 0.5 mile) for our time checks—and having to key in other increments at speed changes—we can arrange to put that whole burden on the calculator. This means that the only distance we shall ever have to key in is the distance according to our odometer.

How do we accomplish that? Simply by issuing the calculator the appropriate orders: "From the odometer distance just keyed in, subtract the previous distance; then calculate the allowed time for the difference, add that time to the previously accumulated time and display the totals."

Of course, right at the start of a leg, when we make our first time check, say for 1 mile, there is no previously entered distance or previously calculated time. So the calculator dutifully subtracts 0 from 1, gets 1 for the answer, calculates the allowed time for 1 mile and adds it to 0. When we call for a time check at 2 miles, the calculator subtracts 1 from 2, figures the allowed time for the difference (the 1-mile increment) and adds it to the time allowed for the first mile. When we key in 3 for a check at 3 miles, the calculator takes 2 from 3 and adds on the time for another mile.

Encountering the speed-change at 3.75 miles, we key in 3.75 and run the program. This time the calculator subtracts 3 from 3.75 and adds on the time for 0.75 mile. Now we store the new speed, and now we can press 4 and run the program again. The calculator subtracts 3.75 from 4, calculates the time for 0.25 mile at the new speed and adds it to the previous total time. At 5 miles—or for that matter at 5.10 or 5.01 or 51 or 501 miles—the same thing happens; *we* deal in total distance, while the calculator works in increments.

That considerable hurdle cleared, we can turn to concocting our navigation programs.

SR-56 AVERAGE-SPEED NAVIGATION PROGRAM I

Calculates allowed time as elapsed (stopwatch) time in minutes and hundredths of minutes

LOC	CODE	KEY	LOC	CODE	KEY	LOC	CODE	KEY
00	74	−	11	02	2	22	64	×
01	34	RCL	12	64	×	23	34	RCL
02	01	1	13	34	RCL	24	04	4
03	94	=	14	04	4	25	94	=
04	35	SUM	15	94	=	26	33	STO
05	01	1	16	35	SUM	27	06	6
06	64	×	17	00	0	28	34	RCL
07	34	RCL	18	34	RCL	29	00	0
08	03	3	19	01	1	30	41	R/S
09	54	÷	20	59	*pause	31	42	RST
10	34	RCL	21	59	*pause			

Data Entries

1. Average speed in miles per hour STO 2
2. 60 STO 3
3. Factor A:

      official length of odometer check ÷ odometer reading at end of check STO 4

---

*Denotes 2nd function key

4. Factor B:
   with Factor A still displayed, press:
   *1/x STO 5

Program Initialization
1. Key in distance in miles (or miles and hundredths) for which the allowed time is wanted
2. RST *fix 2
3. R/S
4. For subsequent time checks key in the distance and press R/S

To Change Average Speed
1. Key in the odometer reading at the speed-change point
2. R/S
3. Key in the new average speed
4. STO 2
5. Key in the next odometer distance for which the allowed time is wanted
6. R/S

For the Odometer Equivalent of an Official Distance
1. Key in the official distance
2. Press × RCL 5 =

Pause (Lose Time)
1. Key in the amount of time to be lost *in minutes and hundredths* (if you have to convert seconds to hundredths of minutes, simply divide the seconds by 60)
2. Press GTO 16 R/S

Gain Time
1. Key in the amount of time to be gained *in minutes and hundredths*
2. Press +/− GTO 16 R/S

Procedure at End of Leg
1. 0 STO 0 STO 1
2. If there is a new average speed, store it in R_2

---

*Denotes 2nd function key

3. Zero odometer and stopwatch
4. Key in the first odometer distance for which the allowed time is wanted and press R/S

Time Displays After One Hour

Note that allowed times of one hour or more will be displayed in minutes: 1 hr. 11.5 min. will be shown as 71.50

Callouts

Between program runs—
RCL 0 displays accumulated allowed time
RCL 1 displays last entered odometer distance
RCL 2 displays the average speed in use
RCL 3 displays 60
RCL 4 displays Factor A
RCL 5 displays Factor B
RCL 6 displays the official-distance equivalent of the distance stored in R_1

How the Program Works

Steps 00 – 03 subtract the previous odometer distance (which at the start of a leg is of course 0.00 miles) from the distance just keyed in; the difference is the distance driven since the previous check.

Steps 04 – 05 add this difference to the distance stored in R_1; R_1 now contains the current distance.

Steps 06 – 08 multiply the distance increment by the constant 60 stored in R_3.

Steps 09 – 11 divide the just-obtained product by the average speed from R_2, giving the uncorrected allowed time for the distance increment.

Steps 12 – 15 multiply the uncorrected allowed time by Factor A (from R_4), giving the corrected allowed time.

Steps 16 – 17 add the allowed time for the distance increment to the total allowed time accumulating in R_0.

Steps 18 – 21 recall and display the total odometer distance.

Steps 22 – 27 multiply the total odometer distance by Factor A (from R_4) and store the equivalent official distance in R_6.

Steps 28 – 29 recall and display the time allowed for the total odometer distance.

Step 30 halts the calculator. (The allowed time remains displayed.)

Step 31, as soon as you key in a new odometer distance and press R/S, sends the calculator back to step 00, where the calculation of the new total allowed time commences.

We will take this program through a sample rally in the next chapter. You can check it out briefly now, though. Store the program in the calculator, verify the keycodes, then load these data:

0 STO 0 STO 1 (this step is not necessary if you know that the contents of R_0 and R_1 are 0)

30 STO 2 (average speed is 30 mph)

60 STO 3 (constant 60)

Factor A: assume an odometer check of 10.00 official miles and an odometer reading of 10.13 miles; then:

10 ÷ 10.13 = STO 4 (stores Factor A)

Factor B: with Factor A still displayed in R_x:

*1/x STO 5 (stores Factor B)

*fix 2 (fixes two decimal places)

RST (sets program counter to 00)

Now you are ready to check allowed times, mile by mile:

1 R/S displays 1.00 (mile), then 1.97 (min.)

2 R/S displays 2.00 (miles), then 3.95 (min.)

3 R/S displays 3.00 (miles), then 5.92 (min.)

Assume that a speed change to 28.85 mph comes at 3.05 miles:

3.05 R/S displays 3.05 (miles), then 6.02 (min.)

Press 28.85 STO 2; then:

4 R/S displays 4.00 (miles), then 7.97 (min.)

5 R/S displays 5.00 (miles), then 10.03 (min.)

And so on.

OK—but you'd like to have the allowed times given in minutes and seconds as well as in minutes and hundredths. Then you want an amended program.

SR-56 AVERAGE-SPEED NAVIGATION PROGRAM IA

Calculates allowed time as elapsed (stopwatch) time
in minutes and hundredths of minutes and
in minutes and seconds

---

*Denotes 2nd function key

LOC	CODE	KEY	LOC	CODE	KEY	LOC	CODE	KEY
00	74	−	17	00	0	34	12	INV
01	34	RCL	18	34	RCL	35	29	*Int
02	01	1	19	01	1	36	64	×
03	94	=	20	59	*pause	37	92	.
04	35	SUM	21	59	*pause	38	06	6
05	01	1	22	64	×	39	94	=
06	64	×	23	34	RCL	40	39	*EXC
07	34	RCL	24	04	4	41	09	9
08	03	3	25	94	=	42	29	*Int
09	54	÷	26	33	STO	43	84	+
10	34	RCL	27	06	6	44	34	RCL
11	02	2	28	34	RCL	45	09	9
12	64	×	29	00	0	46	94	=
13	34	RCL	30	59	*pause	47	41	R/S
14	04	4	31	59	*pause	48	42	RST
15	94	=	32	33	STO			
16	35	SUM	33	09	9			

The data entries for Program IA are exactly the same as those for Program I; indeed, the first thirty steps of the two programs are identical. Steps 30 − 31 display the decimal-minutes time. Steps 32 − 33 store this time in R_9. With the decimal-minutes time still in R_x, steps 34 − 39 pluck out the fractional part—the hundredths of minutes—and multiply it by .6, converting the hundredths to seconds and placing this value to the right of the decimal point for display purposes. Steps 40 − 41 simultaneously place this number in R_9 and retrieve from R_9 the original minutes-and-hundredths time. Step 42 discards the hundredths, preserving the integer—the whole-minutes value. Steps 43 − 46 add to the whole minutes the seconds fraction from R_9, finally displaying the allowed time as minutes, decimal point, seconds.

To see how the answers come out, enter Program IA and the same data you used to check Program I. Now your time checks will look like this:

1 R/S	display:	1.00 (mile)	1.97 (min.)	1.58 (min/sec)
2 R/S	display:	2.00 (miles)	3.95 (min.)	3.57 (min/sec)
3 R/S	display:	3.00 (miles)	5.92 (min.)	5.55 (min/sec)

*Denotes 2nd function key

You've changed your mind again and decided that you don't want to rally on stopwatch time after all. You want to use a chronograph and run on time of day. You're lucky, because the SR-56 can just be made to do the trick in an even hundred program steps, which is all there is; there ain't no more. The program is long and complicated because the SR-56—alas!—offers no kwik'n'e-zee way of converting decimal hours to hours, minutes and seconds.

SR-56 AVERAGE-SPEED NAVIGATION PROGRAM II

Calculates allowed time as clock time (time of day) in hours, minutes and seconds

LOC	CODE	KEY	LOC	CODE	KEY	LOC	CODE	KEY
00	74	–	25	29	*Int	50	33	STO
01	34	RCL	26	64	×	51	00	0
02	01	1	27	06	6	52	34	RCL
03	94	=	28	00	0	53	01	1
04	35	SUM	29	53	)	54	59	*pause
05	01	1	30	33	STO	55	64	×
06	54	÷	31	09	9	56	34	RCL
07	34	RCL	32	29	*Int	57	04	4
08	02	2	33	64	×	58	94	=
09	64	×	34	92	•	59	33	STO
10	34	RCL	35	00	0	60	06	6
11	04	4	36	01	1	61	34	RCL
12	94	=	37	53	)	62	00	0
13	35	SUM	38	84	+	63	41	R/S
14	03	3	39	52	(	64	42	RST
15	34	RCL	40	34	RCL	65	33	STO
16	03	3	41	09	9	66	09	9
17	33	STO	42	12	INV	67	29	*Int
18	09	9	43	29	*Int	68	84	+
19	29	*Int	44	64	×	69	52	(
20	84	+	45	92	•	70	34	RCL
21	52	(	46	00	0	71	09	9
22	34	RCL	47	00	0	72	12	INV
23	09	9	48	06	6	73	29	*Int
24	12	INV	49	94	=	74	64	×

*Denotes 2nd function key

LOC	CODE	KEY	LOC	CODE	KEY	LOC	CODE	KEY
75	01	1	83	06	6	92	54	÷
76	00	0	84	00	0	93	03	3
77	00	0	85	53	)	94	06	6
78	53	)	86	84	+	95	94	=
79	33	STO	87	52	(	96	35	SUM
80	09	9	88	34	RCL	97	03	3
81	29	*Int	89	09	9	98	41	R/S
82	54	÷	90	12	INV	99	42	RST
			91	29	*Int			

The memory registers are used thus:

R_0 contains the time of day, in hours, minutes and seconds, when you should have covered the odometer distance in R_1

R_1 contains the latest-entered odometer distance

R_2 stores the average speed in use

R_3 contains the latest allowed time as decimal hours

R_4 stores Factor A

R_5 stores Factor B

R_6 contains the official-distance equivalent of the odometer distance in R_1

R_7 and R_8 are not used

R_9 is used in the calculations

This is how the program works:

Steps 00 − 14 calculate the corrected allowed time increment in—note carefully, please!—*decimal hours* and add it to the decimal-hours clock time accumulating in R_3.

Steps 15 − 51 convert the decimal-hours time value in R_3 to hours-minutes-seconds clock time and place this value in R_0 in the form HH.MMSS (hours, decimal point, minutes, seconds).

Steps 52 − 54 display the odometer distance from R_1.

Steps 55 − 60 calculate and store in R_6 the official distance.

Steps 61 − 63 display the time of day from R_0 and halt the calculator.

After you have keyed in the next odometer distance for which you want the time, step 64 returns the calculator to step 00, and the new calculation begins.

---

*Denotes 2nd function key

Steps 65 — 97 convert, *when required*, hours-minutes-seconds time to decimal-hours time and add the result to the decimal-hours value in R_3. This part of the program is used only to enter the car's time-of-day starting time and to add pauses and subtract gains that are expressed in hours, minutes and seconds.

Step 98 halts the calculator; step 99 returns the calculator to step 00.

Check the operation of this program by running a hypothetical short first leg with these instructions:

Your starting time (for some inexplicable reason) is 9:07:30 a.m. (7 minutes 30 seconds past 9)

The odometer check is 10.00 official miles; the allowed-time for it is 19 minutes

At end of odometer check start average speed 30.5 mph

At Point A pause for 2 minutes 22 seconds

At Point B change average speed to 36 mph

At Point C gain 3/10 minute

1. Enter the program and carefully check the keycodes.
2. Press *fix 4 to fix four decimal places.
3. Key in and convert your assigned starting time: 9.073 GTO 65 R/S places in R_3 and displays the time as 9.1250 decimal hours.
4. Verify the conversion, if you wish, by pressing GTO 15 R/S. The display will first show 0.0000 (miles)—you haven't gone anywhere yet—and then 9.0730 (your h/m/s starting time, which is now stored in R_0).
5. Drive the 10.00 official miles to the end of the odometer check. Your odometer reads 9.98. Calculate and store your correction factors.
    Factor A: 10 ÷ 9.98 = STO 4
    Factor B: *1/x STO 5
6. Store the average speed you are going to use:
    30.5 STO 2
7. Now you have to add 19 minutes to your starting time. Of course you could have entered 9.2630 instead of 9.0730 at

---

*Denotes 2nd function key

150

step 3, but you didn't, so now key in .19 GTO 65 R/S. The display shows that 0.3167 hour has been added to R_3.

8. Now it's time to match the empty distance register, R_1, with your odometer reading. Key in 9.98 STO 1. You are now ready to go.
9. Check for 10 miles:
    pressing 10 RST R/S displays 10.0000 (miles), then 9.2632 (time of day).
10. Proceeding:
    11 R/S displays 11.000, then 9.2831.
11. Point A comes up at 12.43 miles:
    12.43 R/S displays 12.4300, then 9.3120.
    To add the pause of 2 min. 22 sec., press .0222 GTO 65 R/S; this operation adds 0.0394 hour to R_3.
    Press 12.43 R/S again; the display is 12.4300, then 9.3342.
12. Proceeding:
    13 R/S displays 13.0000, then 9.3449.
    14 R/S displays 14.000, then 9.3647.
13. Point B appears at 14.03 miles:
    14.03 R/S displays 14.0300, then 9.3651.
    To change speed press 36 STO 2.
14. To get on time at 14.5 miles:
    14.5 R/S displays 14.5000, then 9.3738.
15. Point C comes at 17.80 miles:
    17.8 R/S displays 17.8000, then 9.4309.
    In order to gain 3/10 minute you must subtract the decimal-hour equivalent from R_3. This you can do in either of two ways. One is to multiply 0.3 by 0.006 and go through the conversion routine:
    Press .3 × .006 = +/− GTO 65 R/S
    The other way is to divide 0.3 by 60 and subtract the result from R_3 directly:
    Press .3 ÷ 60 = INV SUM 3
    In either case the allowed time in R_3 is reduced by 0.0050 hr. Now if you press 17.8 R/S again, you will see that your time has been set back by 18 seconds, to 9.4251.

16. At 22 miles you round a bend and see the checkpoint ahead:
      22 R/S displays 22.000, then 9.4952.
   Being right on time, you hold your speed and cross the timing line at 22.08 miles by your odometer.
      22.08 R/S displays 22.0800, then 9.4960, which, owing to the peculiarities of rounding, you will have to interpret as 49 minutes and 60 seconds past 9 o'clock, or 9:50:00 a.m.
17. If you wish to check the official distance, pressing RCL 6 gives it: 22.1242 miles.
18. To get ready for the next leg you have several things to do:
    a. Zero your odometer at the restart line
    b. Press 0 STO 1 STO 3 to clear your distance- and time-accumulating registers
    c. If there is a new average speed, store it in R_2
    d. If you have reason to refine your odometer correction factors, do so now:
       official ÷ indicated = STO 4 *1/x STO 5
    e. Enter your assigned leaving time for leg 2, as:
       9.53 GTO 65 R/S
       (Then pressing 0 R/S will verify your out time, giving it as 9.5260)
    And you are ready to go again.

If you want to rally on time of day but prefer hours and decimal minutes to hours, minutes and seconds, there is a program to suit your needs exactly, and of course there are timepieces to match.

SR-56 AVERAGE-SPEED RALLY
NAVIGATION PROGRAM IIA

Calculates allowed time as clock time (time of day)
in hours, minutes and hundredths of minutes

LOC	CODE	KEY	LOC	CODE	KEY	LOC	CODE	KEY
00	74	−	04	35	SUM	08	02	2
01	34	RCL	05	01	1	09	64	×
02	01	1	06	54	÷	10	34	RCL
03	94	=	07	34	RCL	11	04	4

*Denotes 2nd function key

LOC	CODE	KEY	LOC	CODE	KEY	LOC	CODE	KEY
12	94	=	30	94	=	48	41	R/S
13	35	SUM	31	33	STO	49	42	RST
14	03	3	32	00	0	50	33	STO
15	34	RCL	33	34	RCL	51	09	9
16	03	3	34	04	4	52	29	*Int
17	33	STO	35	64	×	53	39	*EXC
18	09	9	36	34	RCL	54	09	9
19	29	*Int	37	01	1	55	12	INV
20	39	*EXC	38	49	*fix	56	29	*Int
21	09	9	39	02	2	57	54	÷
22	12	INV	40	59	*pause	58	92	•
23	29	*Int	41	94	=	59	06	6
24	64	×	42	33	STO	60	84	+
25	92	•	43	06	6	61	34	RCL
26	06	6	44	34	RCL	62	09	9
27	84	+	45	00	0	63	22	GTO
28	34	RCL	46	49	*fix	64	01	1
29	09	9	47	04	4	65	02	2

The memory registers are used thus:

R_0 contains the time of day, in hours, minutes and hundredths of minutes, when you should have covered the odometer distance in R_1

R_1 contains the latest-entered odometer distance

R_2 stores the average speed in use

R_3 contains the latest allowed time as decimal hours

R_4 stores Factor A

R_5 stores Factor B

R_6 contains the official-distance equivalent of the odometer distance in R_1

R_7 and R_8 are not used

R_9 is used in the calculations

How Program IIA works

Steps 00–14 calculate the corrected allowed time increment in decimal hours and add it to the decimal-hours clock time accumulating in R_3.

---
*Denotes 2nd function key

Steps 15–32 convert the decimal-hours time value in R_3 to hours-minutes-hundredths clock time and place this time in R_0 in the form HH.MMmm (hours, decimal point, minutes, hundredths of minutes).

Steps 33–37 multiply Factor A by the current odometer distance in R_1; steps 38–40 display the odometer distance to two decimal places; steps 41–43 place the official-distance equivalent in R_6.

Steps 44–48 recall the allowed time and display it to the necessary four decimal places.

Step 49 returns the calculator to step 00.

When needed for pauses and gains, steps 50-65 convert hours (if any) and decimal minutes to decimal hours; the transfer to step 12 (from steps 64–65) adds the pause to (or subtracts the gain from) R_3 and runs that value through the mill to step 48. Yes, it looks like a rather roundabout process, and it is. You simply have to keep in mind the rationale: You can make the calculator *display* mixed values in just about any way you like, but you can make it do arithmetic only on values that are unmixed. It will not add hours, minutes and seconds any sooner than it will add yards, feet and inches or minims, drams and ounces.

Check out Program IIA using the same instructions you used in checking Program II:

1. Enter the program and verify the keycodes.
2. Key in your assigned starting time as hours, decimal point, minutes and hundredths:

    9.075 GTO 50 R/S first displays 0.00 (miles), then 9.0750 (hours, minutes and hundredths). If you now press RCL 3 you will see that R_3 contains your starting time as 9.1250— that is, $9^{1,250}/_{10,000}$ hours.

3. Calculate Factors A and B as before:
    Factor A: 10 ÷ 9.98 = STO 4
    Factor B: *1/x STO 5
4. Store the first average speed:
    30.5 STO 2

---

*Denotes 2nd function key

5. Add the allowed 19 minutes to your starting time:
    .19 GTO 50 R/S displays 0.00 (miles), then 9.2650
    —9 hours 26.5 minutes; this takes care of the
    odometer check time.
6. Adjust the distance in R_1 to match your odometer reading:
    9.98 STO 1
7. Check for 10 miles:
    10 RST R/S displays 10.00 (miles), then 9.2654 (hours and decimal minutes).
8. Proceeding:
    11 R/S displays 11.00, then 9.2851.
9. Point A comes up at 12.43 miles:
    12.43 R/S displays 12.43, then 9.3133.
    To add the pause of 2 min. 22 sec. you must convert the 22 seconds to hundredths of a minute, then add the whole minutes:
    Press .22 ÷ 60 =+ .02 = GTO 50 R/S; this adds 0.0394 hour to R_3 and displays 12.43 (miles), then 9.3370 (minutes and hundredths).
10. Proceeding:
    13 R/S displays 13.00, then 9.3482.
    14 R/S displays 14.00, then 9.3679.
11. Point B appears at 14.03 miles.
    14.03 R/S displays 14.03, then 9.3685.
    To change speed press 36 STO 2.
12. Now get on time at 14.5 miles:
    14.5 R/S displays 14.50, then 9.3763.
13. Point C comes at 17.80 miles:
    17.8 R/S displays 17.80, then 9.4315.
    In order to gain 3/10 minute here, you must subtract the decimal-hour equivalent from R_3. You can manage it in either of two ways. One is to run 0.0030 through the conversion routine:
    .003 +/− GTO 50 R/S displays 17.80, then 9.4285.
    The alternative is to divide 0.3 by 60 and subtract the result (0.005) from R_3 directly:
    .3 ÷ 60 = INV SUM 3

In either case the allowed time in R₃ is reduced by five one-thousandths of an hour. Press 17.8 R/S again; the display is 17.80, then 9.4285.

14. At 22 miles you approach the checkpoint:
22 R/S displays 22.00, then 9.4986.
On time, you maintain your speed and cross the timing line at 22.08 odometer miles:
22.08 R/S displays 22.08, then 9.4999, which is as near as makes no difference to 9:50, which was the time allowed for this leg according to hours-minutes-seconds Program II.

But, you may protest, 9.4999 is one penalty point removed from 9.5000. All right, let's try to dispose, once and for all, of the mostly invisible, and therefore virtually indiscernible, arithmetical caprices that, depending on which approach you take to solving a problem, may give slightly different answers. There is always the question of your methodology vis-a-vis that of the rally officials; for example, how many decimal places do the rallymaster's calculations preserve? There are the vagaries of rounding—not to mention those of *not* rounding. And let us not even dream of preoccupying ourselves with the theories of significant figures, fascinating though they are.

Of all the interwoven links in the average-speed-rally chain—measuring the distances, measuring the time, performing the calculations and driving to the speed—the calculations are the most precise element. Let's acknowledge what we all know: that when we score a one-point penalty, we have rallied very well—and have been extremely lucky. When we score a zero, we have rallied very well and have been phenomenally lucky. Consider that misreading your odometer by a carlength at the end of a ten-mile check will, at moderate speeds, induce an error of a hundredth of a minute in about twenty miles, and then contemplate what happens to your recorded distance when you pull out to pass another car.

Time-Based Route Directions

A "time-based" rally instruction is one that defines an action point in terms of elapsed time. For example: "The average speed is 30 mph. Exactly 20 1/2 minutes after starting this leg, turn right."

Obviously you are going to want to know what your odometer should read after 20 1/2 minutes have passed. As far as you can tell at the beginning, it will be 30 × 20.5 ÷ 60 = 10.25 official miles, but you must expect to encounter various speed changes, pauses or gains that will require you to update your calculations.

SR-56 Navigational Programs I and IA can readily be modified to successively reestimate the critical distance. You merely tack on a 24-step program supplement in program locations 51 — 74, store the key time (in minutes, decimal point, hundredths of minutes) in R_7, and call in this supplementary routine at every speed change, pause or gain. The answer will be the latest revised corrected odometer reading at the action point.

To store the routine, have the calculator in calculate mode and press GTO 51 LRN and key in the 24 steps, then press LRN again; finally, pressing RST will set the program counter at step 00 of the navigational program. Be sure to store the key time in R_7 as decimal minutes.

SR-56 SUPPLEMENTARY ROUTINE FOR TIME-BASED INSTRUCTIONS

Calculates the odometer reading at which a time-identified action point will be found

(For use in conjunction with Program I or IA)

LOC	CODE	KEY	LOC	CODE	KEY	LOC	CODE	KEY
50			58	64	×	67	05	5
51	52	(	59	52	(	68	53	)
52	34	RCL	60	34	RCL	69	84	+
53	07	7	61	02	2	70	34	RCL
54	74	−	62	54	÷	71	01	1
55	34	RCL	63	34	RCL	72	94	=
56	00	0	64	03	3	73	41	R/S
57	53	)	65	64	×	74	42	RST
			66	34	RCL			

How the time-based-instruction routine works:

Steps 51 − 57 calculate the amount of time remaining.

Steps 58 − 64 multiply the remaining time by the current average speed and divide the product by 60, giving the uncorrected distance for that time at that speed.

Steps 65 – 67 correct the calculated distance for odometer error.

Steps 68 – 72 add the corrected distance to the distance previously driven. The result displayed at step 73 is the projected odometer reading (which is always subject to subsequent revision) where the time-based instruction is to be executed.

Step 74 returns the calculator to step 00 of the navigational program in use.

To call in the supplemental routine at any time simply press GTO 51 R/S.

The key time *must* be stored in R_7 as minutes, decimal point, hundredths of minutes. For example, a key time of 29 1/2 minutes is stored thus: 29.5 STO 7. If the key time is 1 hour 29 minutes 33 seconds, convert the seconds to hundredths of minutes and add the whole minutes: 33 ÷ 60 + 89 = STO 7.

The supplementary routine should be run at least once before and after every speed change, pause and gain; the keystrokes are GTO 51 R/S. (Running this routine has no effect on the average-speed calculations, nor does it change the contents of any of the storage registers.)

To see exactly how the time-based-instruction routine works, assume these directions at the beginning of a leg:

Your average speed is 33 mph.
At point A change speed to 37 mph.
At Point B gain 10 seconds
At Point C change speed to 29 mph.
At Point D pause for 15 seconds.
Turn right 19 minutes 11 seconds after starting this leg.

You elect to run with Program IA? Very well; load it and check the keycodes. Now with the calculator in calculate mode, press GTO 51 LRN and load the time-based supplementary routine. Load the parameters, assuming, for simplicity's sake, no odometer error:

33 STO 2
60 STO 3
1 STO 4 STO 5
11 ÷ 60 + 19 = STO 7
*fix 2 RST

---
*Denotes 2nd function key

The action points appear at these distances:

A—2.46 miles   C—7.01 miles
B—4.93 miles   D—9.84 miles

Here are your keystrokes and displays for the leg, including the necessary calculations and recalculations of the time-based distance:

	Displays		
Keystrokes	miles	dec. min.	min./sec.
1 R/S	1.00	1.82	1.49
2 R/S	2.00	3.64	3.38
GTO 51 R/S	10.55		
2.46 R/S	2.46	4.47	4.28
37 STO 2			
GTO 51 R/S	11.53		
3 R/S	3.00	5.35	5.21
4 R/S	4.00	6.97	6.58
4.93 R/S	4.93	8.48	8.29
10 ÷ 60 = INV SUM 0			
4.93 R/S	4.93	8.31	8.19
GTO 51 R/S	11.63		
5 R/S	5.00	8.42	8.25
6 R/S	6.00	10.05	10.03
7.01 R/S	7.01	11.68	11.41
29 STO 2			
GTO 51 R/S	10.63		
8 R/S	8.00	13.71	13.44
9 R/S	9.00	15.80	15.48
9.84 R/S	9.84	17.54	17.32
15 ÷ 60 = SUM 0			
GTO 51 R/S	10.51		
10 R/S	10.00	18.12	18.07
Finally, as verification:			
10.51 R/S	10.51	19.18	19.11

And you turn right at 10.51 miles.

What happens if the key time is measured not from the beginning of a leg but from the moment you are due to arrive at some intermediate point? The complication proves to be extremely minor. Consider these route instructions:

Your average speed is 30.00 mph.
Follow the road you are on.
At Point A change average speed to 36.00 mph.
At Point B turn left; 17 minutes 20 seconds after your allowed time to Point B turn right.

Switch the calculator off, then on, and load SR-56 Navigational Program I and the Supplementary Routine for Time-based Instructions. For simplicity's sake assume no odometer error; store 1 in R_4 and R_5. Store 30 in R_2 and 60 in R_3. Press *fix 2.

Point A comes at 3.00 miles, Point B at 5.35 miles. Then:

Keystrokes	Display Miles	Minutes
1 RST R/S	1.00	2.00
2 R/S	2.00	4.00
3 R/S	3.00	6.00
36 STO 2		
4 R/S	4.00	7.67
5 R/S	5.00	9.33
5.35 R/S	5.35	9.92

Now you have to store the key time in R_7, and in decimal minutes. That key time is the allowed time to here plus 17 min. 20 sec. The time to here, the 5.35-mile point, is already displayed as 9.92 minutes; 17 min. 20 sec. is 17.33 minutes. So with 9.92 displayed, press + 17.33 = STO 7 to store 27.25 minutes in R_7. Now press GTO 51 R/S. The display gives you the projected distance after an additional 17 min. 20 sec.: 15.75 miles. If any further speed changes or pauses or gains take place, handle them routinely, resorting to the supplemental routine each time.

Obviously, there is no room for another two dozen steps in Program IIA. If, then, while conning your route directions you discover a time-based instruction, you will probably want to switch to one of the other programs.

---

*Denotes 2nd function key

Simultaneous Displays

If you insist on seeing the distance and time displayed together, the SR-56 will oblige—but you must be prepared to imagine where one of the two decimal points goes. To achieve the simultaneous display, we multiply the distance (from R_1) by 10^5 (100,000), thus moving the significant digits well to the left; then we add to it the allowed time (from R_0). The result is a contrived number in which the single decimal point appears near the right-hand end, as part of the allowed-time value. Here is the SR-56 basic navigation program altered to give a simultaneous display:

SR-56 AVERAGE-SPEED NAVIGATION PROGRAM I MODIFIED FOR SIMULTANEOUS DISPLAY OF DISTANCE AND TIME

Calculates allowed time as elapsed (stopwatch) time in minutes and hundredths of mintues

LOC	CODE	KEY	LOC	CODE	KEY
00	74	—			
01	34	RCL	19	01	1
02	01	1	20	64	×
03	94	=	21	34	RCL
04	35	SUM	22	04	4
05	01	1	23	94	=
06	64	×	24	33	STO
07	34	RCL	25	06	6
08	03	3	26	34	RCL
09	54	÷	27	01	1
10	34	RCL	28	64	×
11	02	2	29	05	5
12	64	×	30	19	*10^x
13	34	RCL	31	84	+
14	04	4	32	34	RCL
15	94	=	33	00	0
16	35	SUM	34	94	=
17	00	0	35	41	R/S
18	34	RCL	36	42	RST

*Denotes 2nd function key

The minutes-and-seconds program can be similarly treated:

SR-56 AVERAGE-SPEED NAVIGATION PROGRAM IA MODIFIED FOR SIMULTANEOUS DISPLAY OF DISTANCE AND TIME

Calculates allowed time as elapsed (stopwatch) time in minutes and seconds

LOC	CODE	KEY	LOC	CODE	KEY	LOC	CODE	KEY
00	74	−	17	00	0	34	33	STO
01	34	RCL	18	34	RCL	35	09	9
02	01	1	19	01	1	36	12	INV
03	94	=	20	64	×	37	29	*Int
04	35	SUM	21	34	RCL	38	64	×
05	01	1	22	04	4	39	92	.
06	64	×	23	94	=	40	06	6
07	34	RCL	24	33	STO	41	53	)
08	03	3	25	06	6	42	39	*Exc
09	54	÷	26	34	RCL	43	09	9
10	34	RCL	27	01	1	44	29	*Int
11	02	2	28	64	×	45	84	+
12	64	×	29	05	5	46	34	RCL
13	34	RCL	30	19	*10^x	47	09	9
14	04	4	31	84	×	48	94	=
15	94	=	32	34	RCL	49	41	R/S
16	35	SUM	33	00	0	50	42	RST

Data entries, program initialization and everything else are exactly the same as for Program I. It is especially important here not to overlook *fix 2 to fix two decimal places.

How the simultaneous-display programs work:

Modified Programs I and IA are largely the same as the original programs except for the insertion of new steps 26 − 32. These seven steps retrieve the odometer distance from R_1 and multiply it by 10^5, moving the value—without a decimal point—to the extreme left of the display. Using the exponent-of-10 key effects the multiplication in two steps, whereas keying in 100000 would use six steps.

---

*Denotes 2nd function key

Chapter 12
Testing the
SR-56 Rally Programs

YOU ARE NOW going to rally with the SR-56 and SR-56 Program I, the basic 32-step minutes-and-hundredths program. Your hypothetical equipment for this imaginary even will be minimal: a nonreversing hundredths-reading odometer, a hundredths-reading stopwatch, plenty of pencils and paper (adequate notes of times and distances along the way are vital), a kitchen table and a copy of this book. You will enjoy the instructions, because for once you have no route to follow. (The cumulative mileages in parentheses are *your* odometer readings.)

1. Your car number is 7, and your starting time is 9 a.m. plus your car number in minutes. (*00.00 miles*)
2. The length of the odometer check is 20.00 official miles; you are allowed 37 1/2 minutes for this run. (*20.07 miles*)
3. Proceed from the end of the odometer check at the average speed equivalent to that allowed for the check run.
4. Exactly 5 miles after leaving the end of the odometer check increase your average speed by 10%.
5. Within 2 miles after traffic light (*27.27 miles*) pause for 2 minutes 18 seconds.
6. At T change average speed to 43.2 mph. (*31.99 miles*)
7. At stop sign (*38.78 miles*) change average speed to 24 mph and suppose that a phantom car has left this point 3 minutes

before you were due to arrive here. The phantom car's average speed is 20 mph. At the point where you overtake the phantom car, turn right and change your average speed to 34.5 mph.
8. Turn left 45.67 miles from the start of the rally.
9. Within 4 miles after having executed instruction 8 gain 40 seconds.
10. At T reduce average speed by 10%. (*54.08 miles*)
11. After passing red barn turn left.

Switch on the calculator, press LRN and load SR-56 Average-Speed Program I. Press LRN RST LRN and verify the keycodes, using the SST key. Correct any incorrectly entered program steps and check again. When you are sure you have the program stored correctly, again press LRN RST. The program counter is now set at 00.

Zero your imaginary odometer and your imaginary stopwatch. Listen carefully for the imaginary time signal. At 9:07 start your stopwatch and take off.

As you read through the instructions you discover that for instruction 3 you will have to determine the average speed allowed for the odometer check: 20 miles in 37 1/2 minutes. Press 20 × 60 ÷ 37.5 = . The answer is 32 mph. Make a note.

While proceeding briskly but decorously through the odometer check, you might wish to deal with instruction 7. You will find in the Appendix the formula you need where a phantom car started going away from you E minutes ago:

$$D = \frac{A \times B \times E}{60(B - A)}$$

where A = speed of phantom car in miles per hour
B = speed of rally car in miles per hour
D = miles rally car must travel to catch phantom car
E = minutes phantom car is ahead at start

In this case, $A = 20$ (mph)
$B = 24$ (mph)
$E = 3$ (minutes)

Substituting these values in the equation:

$$D = \frac{20 \times 24 \times 3}{60(24 - 20)}$$

The calculator is in calculate mode, so press 20 × 24 × 3 ÷ (60 × (24 − 20 =. The answer is 6 miles. That is 6 official miles; but until you complete the odometer check and establish your odometer difference, you can only note the official distance and convert it to odometer distance later.

At the 20.00-mile marker you find that your odometer reads 20.07—slightly slow. Now you can make your data entries, with the calculator still in calculate mode, of course:

32 STO 2	Average speed in R_2
60 STO 3	Constant 60 in R_3
20 ÷ 20.07 = STO 4	Factor A in R_4
*1/x STO 5	Factor B in R_5
*fix 2	Fixes 2-decimal-place display
RST	Program counter at 00

Now for your first run of the program:

20.07 R/S displays   20.07 (miles)
                               37.50 (minutes)

If you want to make a check every half mile, it's easy enough:

21.5 R/S displays   21.50 (miles)
                              40.17 (minutes)

You had better be getting ready for instruction 4 by finding out how far 25 official miles will be according to your odometer:

25 × RCL 5 = displays   25.09 (miles)

And the new speed:

RCL 2 + CE × .1 = displays 35.20 (mph)

Make notes.

Don't forget that in executing instruction 7 you'll have to know your odometer's equivalent of 6 official miles:

6 × RCL 5 = displays   6.02 (miles)

---

*Denotes 2nd function key

At 25 miles make a time check, and at 25.09 miles change speed:

25 R/S displays	25.00 (miles)
	46.71 (minutes)
25.09 R/S displays	25.09 (miles)
	46.88 (minutes)

35.2 STO 2 stores the new speed in R_2

Check your time at the next half mile:

25.5 R/S displays	25.50 (miles)
	47.58 (minutes)

Again:

26 R/S displays	26.00 (miles)
	48.43 (minutes)

The traffic light in instruction 5 appears at 27.27 miles.

27.27 R/S displays	27.27 (miles)
	50.58 (minutes)

Hereabouts you are to add a pause of 2 minutes 18 seconds to your allowed running time. Remember that it is mandatory to key in that time as minutes and hundredths:

18 ÷ 60 + 2 = displays	2.30 (minutes)
GTO 16 R/S displays	27.27 (miles)
	52.88 (minutes)

(NOTE: If you were using Program IA, GTO 16 would be correct here also. Program II, however, handles pauses and gains somewhat differently, as has already been explained.)

The distance reading has not changed, but 2.3 minutes have been added to the allowed time.

Now you have a free zone of 2 × RCL 5 = 2.01 miles, at the end of which you want to be exactly on time, so:

RCL 1 + 2.01 = R/S displays	29.28 (miles)
	56.30 (minutes)

You continue on the average speed, making regular time checks, until you come to the T in instruction 6. Your odometer reads 31.99 miles. Change speed to 43.2 mph:

31.99 R/S displays   31.99 (miles)
                                               60.90 (minutes)

43.2 STO 2 stores the new speed in R_2

Press on, making more checks, until you reach the stop sign in instruction 7. Your odometer reads 38.78 miles.

38.78 R/S displays   38.78 (miles)
                                               70.30 (minutes)

24 STO 2 stores the new speed in R_2

Your notes tell you that you have 6.02 miles to go at this speed. Then RCL 1 + 6.02 = reveals that the speed change called for at the end of instruction 7 will occur at 44.80 miles according to your odometer.

While puttering along at 24 mph, meanwhile, you will want to anticipate the left turn in instruction 8. To find out how far 45.67 official miles will read on your odometer, 45.67 × RCL 5 = tells you: 45.83 miles. Make a note.

At 44.80 miles, turn right and change speed to 34.5 mph:

44.8 R/S displays   44.80 (miles)
                                               85.30 (minutes)

34.5 STO 2 stores the new speed in R_2

Verify your time on the even mile (45), turn left at 45.83 miles and prepare to gain 40 seconds as instruction 9 directs:

45.83 R/S displays   45.83 (miles)
                                             87.08 (minutes)

In case you don't know that 40 seconds is 2/3 or 0.67 minute, work it out: 40 ÷ 60 = 0.67. Since this is a gain, your allowed time will be shortened, and so you must change the sign by pressing the +/− key. Now you can press GTO 16 R/S. To sum up:

40 ÷ 60 = +/− GTO 16 R/S displays   45.83 (miles)
                                                          86.41 (minutes)

The time in R_0 has been shortened by 0.67 minute, as desired. Your only concern now is to make up the time before you have completed 49.67 official miles, which is $49.67 \times$ RCL $5 = 49.84$ odometer miles. At that point the time should be:

49.84 R/S displays	49.84 (miles)
	93.36 (minutes)

The T in instruction 10 shows up at 54.08 miles:

54.08 R/S displays	54.08 (miles)
	100.71 (minutes)

There are several different ways to reduce speed by 10%. This one is as good as any:

RCL $2 \times .9 =$ STO 2 does it, displaying 31.05 (mph) and storing it in R_2

Check for 55 miles:

55 R/S displays	55.00 (miles)
	102.48 (minutes)

As you round a bend, looking for a red barn, you see the checkpoint about a tenth of a mile ahead. Your odometer reads 58.60 miles. Check quickly:

58.65 R/S displays	58.65 (miles)
	109.51 (minutes)
58.7 R/S displays	58.70 (miles)
	109.61 (minutes)

And you cross the timing line with your instruments showing that mileage and that time.

If the checkpoint workers hand out a data sheet, and if it shows that you were early or late by an amount of time that you cannot account for, and if you have not been off course, you may want to check your odometer correction factors. According to your odometer, the length of this leg was 58.70 miles. According to the final figure stored in R_6, it was 58.50 official miles. Suppose the data sheet gives the official distance as 58.40 miles and you were a few unaccountable seconds late in finishing. To refine your correction factor, use the standard formula: official distance ÷ odometer distance. In this case the official distance is 58.40 miles, and your indicated distance is 58.70 miles. Pressing 58.4 ÷ 58.7 = STO 4 stores your new Factor A: .9948892675; then *1/x STO 5 stores your new Factor B: 1.005136986. The difference between these new factors and the respective original ones (.9965122073 and 1.0035000000) is less than 8 feet 7 inches in a mile, but over a long distance it adds up.

Before starting the next leg, you must index your equipment:

1. Press 0 STO 0 STO 1 (time and distance revert to zero, and so must these memories).
2. Zero your odometer on the starting line.
3. Zero your stopwatch.
4. If there is a new average speed, store it in R_2.

If you intend to use Program II, the hours-minutes-seconds time-of-day program, some practice at home is highly advisable, for it is a rather complicated routine. Try the sample rally with it and see if you come up with these keystrokes and answers:

1. Load and verify program. Place calculator in execute mode.

2. *fix 4

Display

3. 9.07 GTO 65 R/S   9.1167 (hours)

4. GTO 15 R/S   0.000 (miles)
                               9.0660 (hms)
                               (equivalent to
                               9.0700)
5. 20 × 60 ÷ 37.5 = STO 2   32.0000 (mph)
6. 20 × 24 × 3 ÷ (60 × (24 − 20 =   6.0000 (miles)
7. 20 ÷ 20.07 = STO 4   0.9965
8. *1/x STO 5   1.0035
9. RST   1.0035

---

*Denotes 2nd function key

(cont. from previous page)

		Display
10.	20.07 R/S	20.0700 (miles)
		9.4430 (hms)
11.	21.5 R/S	21.5000 (miles)
		9.4710 (hms)
12.	25 × RCL 5 =	25.0875 (Miles)
13.	RCL 2 + CE × .1 =	35.2000 (mph)
14.	6 × RCL 5 =	6.0210 (miles)
15.	25 R/S	25.0000 (miles)
		9.5343 (hms)
16.	25.09 R/S	25.0900 (miles)
		9.5353 (hms)
17.	35.2 STO 2	35.2000 (mph)
18.	25.5 R/S	25.5000 (miles)
		9.5435 (hms)
19.	26 R/S	26.0000 (miles)
		9.5526 (hms)
20.	27.27 R/S	27.2700 (miles)
		9.5735 (hms)
21.	.0218 GTO 65 R/S	0.0383 (hour)
22.	27.27 R/S	27.2700 (miles)
		9.5953 (hms)
23.	2 × RCL 5 + RCL 1 = R/S	29.2770 (miles)
		10.0318 (hms)
24.	31.99 R/S	31.9900 (miles)
		10.0754 (hms)
25.	43.2 STO 2	43.2000 (mph)
26.	38.78 R/S	38.7800 (miles)
		10.1718 (hms)

	Display
(cont. from previous page)	
27. 24 STO 2	24.0000 (mph)
28. from 14: 6.02 + RCL 1 =	44.8000 (miles)
29. 45.67 × RCL 5 =	45.8298 (miles)
30. 44.8 R/S	44.80000 (miles) 10.3218 (hms)
31. 34.5 STO2	34.5000 (mph)
32. 45 R/S	45.0000 (miles) 10.3239 (hms)
33. from 29: 45.8298 R/S	45.8298 (miles) 10.3405 (hms)
34. .004 +/− GTO 65 R/S	−0.0111 (hour)
35. 45.8298 R/S	45.8298 (miles) 10.3325 (hms)
36. 49.67 × RCL 5 = R/S	49.8438 (miles) 10.4022 (hms)
37. 54.08 R/S	54.08 (miles) 10.4734 (hms)
38. RCL 2 × .9 = STO 2	31.05 (mph)
39. 55 R/S	55.0000 (miles) 10.4929 (hms)
40. 58.65 R/S	58.6500 (miles) 10.5631 (hms)
41. 58.7 R/S	58.7000 (miles) 10.5636 (hms)

If the data sheet gives the allowed time as 1 hour 49 minutes 36 seconds, you have scored a highly desirable zero.

Before starting the next leg, you have a few things to do:
1. Press 0 STO 1 STO 3 (these memories *must* be cleared).
2. Zero your odometer on the starting line.
3. Key in your assigned departure time as hours, decimal point, minutes (and seconds if there happen to be any) and press GTO 65 R/S.
4. Press GTO 15 R/S.
5. If there is a new average speed, store it in R_2.

You may find it interesting to navigate this rally once more, this time using Program IIA, which gives the clock time in decimal minutes.

1. Load and verify Program IIA. Place calculator in execute mode.

	Display
2. 9.07 GTO 50 R/S	0.00 (miles)
	9.0700 (hrs/min)
3. 20 × 60 ÷ 37.5 = STO 2	32.0000 (mph)
4. 20 × 24 × 3 ÷ (60 × (24 − 20 =	6.0000 (miles)
5. 20 ÷ 20.07 = STO 4	0.9965 (Factor A)
6. *1/x STO 5	1.0035 (Factor B)
7. RST	1.0035
8. 20.07 R/S	20.07 (miles)
	9.4450 (h/m)
9. 21.5 R/S	21.50 (miles)
	9.4717 (h/m)
10. 25 × RCL 5 =	25.0875 (miles)
11. RCL 2 + CE × .1 =	35.2000 (mph)
12. 6 × RCL 5 =	6.0210 (miles)
13. 25 R/S	25.00 (miles)
	9.5371 (h/m)
14. 25.09 R/S	25.09 (miles)
	9.5388 (h/m)
15. 35.2 STO 2	35.2000 (mph)
16. 25.5 R/S	25.50 (miles)
	9.5458 (h/m)
17. 26 R/S	26.00 (miles)
	9.5543 (h/m)

*Denotes 2nd function key

	Display
(cont. from previous page)	
18. 27.27 R/S	27.27 (miles)
	9.5758 (h/m)
19. .023 GTO 50 R/S (pause must be keyed in as 2.3 minutes)	27.27 (miles)
	9.5988 (h/m)
20. 2 × RCL 5 + RCL 1 = R/S	29.28 (miles)
	10.0329 (h/m)
21. 31.99 R/S	31.99 (miles)
	10.0790 (h/m)
22. 43.2 STO 2	43.2000 (mph)
23. 38.78 R/S	38.78 (miles)
	10.1730 (h/m)
24. 24 STO 2	24.000 (mph)
25. 6.02 + RCL 1 =	44.8000 (miles)
26. 45.67 × RCL 5 =	45.8298 (miles)
27. 44.8 R/S	44.80 (miles)
	10.3230 (h/m)
28. 34.5 STO 2	34.5000 (mph)
29. 45 R/S	45.00 (miles)
	10.3264 (h/m)
30. 45.8298	45.83 (miles)
	10.3408 (h/m)
31. .0067 +/− GTO 50 R/S	45.83 (miles)
	10.3341 (h/m)
32. 49.67 × RCL 5 =	49.8438 (miles)
33. 54.08 R/S	54.08 (miles)
	10.4771 (h/m)
34. RCL 2 × .9 = STO 2	31.0500 (mph)
35. 55 R/S	55.00 (miles)
	10.4948 (h/m)
36. 58.65 R/S	58.65 (miles)
	10.5651 (h/m)
37. 58.7 R/S	58.70 (miles)
	10.5660 (h/m)

Your calculated time due at the control is the same as before; 10.5660 is 10:56.6, or 10:56:36.

Don't overlook the little formalities that precede the start of the next leg:

1. Press 0 STO 1 STO 3 (it is imperative that these two memories be cleared).
2. Zero your odometer on the starting line.
3. Key in your assigned time out as hours, decimal point, minutes (and hundredths if there should be any) GTO 50 R/S.
4. If there is a new average speed, store it in R_2.

Chapter 13
Unmaking Mistakes

Recovering After Getting Lost

THE BEST ADVICE about getting lost on a rally can be summed up in one word: *don't*! When in doubt about which road to take, you are far better off to stop and waste a few minutes choosing the right one than to plunge dead on time down the wrong one. Like every other rallyist, however, you will get off course now and then, and although the odds against your emerging unscathed are very long, the possibility does exist that once in a great while you'll be lucky. This chapter tells you how to adjust your calculations when you have gone off the route.

Consider a rally leg that starts off with these instructions:

Start at 2:48 p.m. The average speed is 32.4 mph. At 7.77 miles turn left.

You are using SR-56 Program I. Enter it and check the keycodes. Then press 32.4 STO 2 60 STO 3. Assume that at the end of the 20.20-mile odometer check your odometer read 20.44. Press 20.2 ÷ 20.44 = STO 4 *1/x STO 5 *fix 2 RST. At 2:48, your odometer zeroed, you start your minutes-and-hundredths stopwatch and take off.

You check at 1 mile (1.83 min.), 2 miles (3.66 min.), 3 miles (5.49 min.). Just as you press 4 R/S you run from blacktop onto gravel, and this rally is not supposed to have any dirt roads. Somewhere back there you did something wrong.

Your odometer, a nonreversing type, reads 3.89 miles; you write that down. Your driver turns around, wasting as little yardage

---
*Denotes 2nd function key

as possible, and backtracks to the turning you missed. The odometer now reads 4.46 miles. Since you are unable to adjust the mileage in the odometer, you will have to adjust the allowed time in the calculator.

4.46 R/S displays	4.46 (miles)
	8.16 (minutes)

If you had not gone off the route, your time for 4.46 miles would be 8.16 minutes. But now you must reduce your allowed time by the calculated off-course time:

(4.46 − 3.89) × 2 = displays	1.14 (miles) (total off-course distance)
+/− GTO 06 R/S displays*	4.46 (miles)
	6.08 (minutes)

You have deducted 2.08 minutes—the calculated, corrected off-course time. The calculator will continue to give you your compensated time allowed: for 5 miles, 7.06 min., for 6 miles, 8.89 min., and so on.

Besides having to make up for lost time, you need to know where 7.77 official miles is going to be according to your odometer, which has 1.14 too many indicated miles in it:

7.77 × RCL 5 + 1.14 = displays   9.00 (miles)

When your odometer shows 9.00, turn left.

What if you have a reversing (subtracting) or a resettable odometer? If it is truly resettable, as with individual thumbwheels, you would calculate the reading where you went off course:

4.46 − 3.89 = displays	0.57 (half the off-course distance)
+/− + 3.89 = displays	3.32 (original reading at point of error)

and set your odometer to 3.32.

If your odometer can be made to subtract on the run, switch it off, if you can, while turning around, then switch to − (subtract) and drive back to the point of error. There it will read 3.32. Switch back to + (add) and hurry along the right road.

---

*GTO 06 applies as well to all the other SR-56 navigational programs: IA, II and IIA.

In neither case would you adjust the time in the calculator. The rule after getting lost is this: If you can adjust your indicated distance, do so; if you can't, then adjust your calculated time; but whichever you do, adjust only one.

Changing Speed at the Wrong Place

What is the remedy for missing a speed change (as when you overlook the identifying landmark) or for changing speed too soon (as when you misidentify the landmark)? If you have failed to make notes along the way, nothing can help you much. If you have jotted down mileages at all action points, your chances of recovery are as good as the distance to the next checkpoint. If you can provide the data, the calculator will cope with the reconstruction. Consider this instruction:

> Your average speed is 42 mph. At double-track railroad crossing change average speed to 39 mph.

At 10.55 miles by your odometer you cross two railroad rails and there change speed, making a note of the distance. Presently you come to another railroad crossing, this one with four rails . . . four rails, two rails per track, *double track—this* is the intended speed-change point. What to do?

First of all, write down the odometer reading: 13.75 miles. If you are interested in the bad news, $13.75 - 10.55 =$ will give you the distance you have traveled 3 mph too slowly: 3.2 miles. But to get directly to the crucial business at hand:

10.55 R/S	Restores to R_0 and R_1 the allowed time and the indicated distance they contained, respectively, when you changed speed prematurely
42 STO 2	Restores the first average speed to R_2
13.75 R/S	Calculates and displays the correct allowed time at 13.75 miles
39 STO 2	Effects the speed change at 13.75 miles

Now what about *missing* a speed change, as might happen where two separate instructions turn out to be not so separate after all?

> Your average speed is 38 mph. Turn right after stop sign.
> When you enter Smith Road change average speed to 28 mph.

You turn right after the stop sign and continue at 38 mph. Routinely you note the distance: 8.68 miles. Merrily you go along and just as you get ready to check your time for 10 miles you see a sign that makes it all too clear that the name of the road you are on is—Smith Road. You should have lowered your speed back at the stop sign.

First of all you slow down, having driven more than a mile 10 mph too fast. Then you move to correct your figures:

8.68 R/S	Restores R_0 and R_1 to their condition when you turned at the stop sign
28 STO 2	Effects the speed change at the right place
10 R/S	Calculates and displays the corrected allowed time at your present position

Check your timepiece and, at the right moment, resume rallying.

When You've Pressed the Wrong Button

Keystroke mistakes made on the SR-56 are correctable in varying degrees and by different methods. The CE key corrects incorrect number entries (the decimal point included) made through the keyboard; it does so without affecting values recalled from memory or results of calculations. The CE key also stops a flashing display (an indication that some kind of error has been made) without affecting the number displayed or any pending calculations. The CLR key clears not only the display but also all calculations in progress. If you accidentally press a wrong operation key, such as + for − or × for ÷, there are ways to rectify such mistakes without having to go all the way back to the beginning; study the SR-56 Owner's Manual.

Until you have grown thoroughly familar with the calculator and have mastered the tricks of error correction, the best thing to do when your finger slips is to press CLR and start all over again. However, if you key in a wrong mileage and press R/S when you are using a navigation program, no harm is done. Just let the program run, ignore the answer, key in the correct distance and press R/S again. If you do happen to foul up a program, switch the calculator off, reenter the program, verify the keycodes, store the parameters and run quickly through all the significant calculations until you have regained the status quo. It will take only a few minutes *if* you have kept proper notes.

Chapter 14
Rally Scoring
Programs for the SR-56

THE CALCULATOR'S USEFULNESS in rallying is by no means confined to navigators. When it comes time to do the scoring, the SR-56 can work its wonders for the rally officials as well. In your sometime role of scorer you may want a car-by-car calculating routine that stores the constants (the allowed running time for each leg), accepts the variables (each car's starting and finishing times for each leg), calculates the time taken, compares it with the time allowed, calculates the leg scores and adds them up to give each car's total score. A program must of course deal in the same time units that were used to time the event. If there is a maximum late penalty, the calculator must know when to apply it.

On the other hand, you may prefer to score checkpoint by checkpoint—figuring all the cars' scores at Control 1, then all their scores at Control 2, etc. At this writing such a scheme is commonly used in Sports Car Club of America events; moreover, SCCA divisional and national rallies generally specify a five-minute maximum penalty whether a car is late or early. A scoring program meeting these requirements is given at the end of this chapter. This chapter first presents four programs for scoring rallies car-by-car with the aid of the SR-56. All of them will handle as many as six legs, calculating and accumulating penalties for earliness or lateness. Two of the programs (I and IA) use an hours-minutes-seconds time base; the other two (II and IIA) use hours, minutes and hundredths of minutes. Programs I and II score at the flat rate of one penalty point per time unit of error; Programs IA and IIA automatically calculate a prescribed maximum penalty for lateness.

The two flat-rate-penalty (no maximum) programs take advantage of the SR-56's several levels of subroutines to move the calculator along automatically from the calculations for the first leg to those of the second leg, and so on, recalling the allowed time for the next leg to be dealt with. As scorer, you have only to key in the car's starting and finishing times, leg by leg, and press the R/S key.

The two maximum-late-penalty programs require the scorer to guide the calculator from leg to leg. The reason is that the SR-56 needs rather a lot of program steps to accomplish everything that has to be done. Calling the stored allowed times from their storage registers is no great bother, however.

In all four programs, the allowed driving times for the six legs are stored in memories $R_1 - R_6$. The starting and finishing times, leg by leg, are loaded in R_8 and R_9, respectively. R_7 is used for calculating purposes. The score is accumulated, and finally displayed, in R_0.

SR-56 SCORING PROGRAM I

*Scores one car at a time for up to six legs
at one point per second early or late
(no maximum penalty)*

LOC	CODE	KEY	LOC	CODE	KEY	LOC	CODE	KEY
00	34	RCL	13	03	3	26	57	*subr
01	01	1	14	57	*subr	27	03	3
02	57	*subr	15	03	3	28	09	9
03	03	3	16	09	9	29	41	R/S
04	09	9	17	41	R/S	30	34	RCL
05	41	R/S	18	34	RCL	31	06	6
06	34	RCL	19	04	4	32	57	*subr
07	02	2	20	57	*subr	33	03	3
08	57	*subr	21	03	3	34	09	9
09	03	3	22	09	9	35	34	RCL
10	09	9	23	41	R/S	36	00	0
11	41	R/S	24	34	RCL	37	41	R/S
12	34	RCL	25	05	5	38	42	RST

*Denotes 2nd function key

LOC	CODE	KEY	LOC	CODE	KEY	LOC	CODE	KEY
39	57	*subr	59	06	6	80	29	*Int
40	06	6	60	00	0	81	64	×
41	09	9	61	94	=	82	01	1
42	39	*EXC	62	59	*pause	83	00	0
43	08	8	63	59	*pause	84	00	0
44	57	*subr	64	59	*pause	85	53	)
45	06	6	65	28	*|x|	86	33	STO
46	09	9	66	35	SUM	87	07	7
47	35	SUM	67	00	0	88	29	*Int
48	08	8	68	58	*rtn	89	84	+
49	34	RCL	69	33	STO	90	52	(
50	09	9	70	07	7	91	34	RCL
51	57	*subr	71	29	*Int	92	07	7
52	06	6	72	64	×	93	12	INV
53	09	9	73	06	6	94	29	*Int
54	74	−	74	00	0	95	54	÷
55	34	RCL	75	84	+	96	92	.
56	08	8	76	52	(	97	06	6
57	94	=	77	34	RCL	98	94	=
58	64	×	78	07	7	99	58	*rtn
			79	12	INV			

SR-56 SCORING PROGRAM IA

Scores one car at a time for up to six legs at one point per second early or late, with a maximum penalty for lateness

LOC	CODE	KEY	LOC	CODE	KEY	LOC	CODE	KEY
00	57	*subr	09	08	8	18	94	=
01	05	5	10	34	RCL	19	47	*$x \geq t$
02	00	0	11	09	9	20	03	3
03	39	*EXC	12	57	*subr	21	07	7
04	08	8	13	05	5	22	93	+/−
05	57	*subr	14	00	0	23	64	×
06	05	5	15	74	−	24	06	6
07	00	0	16	34	RCL	25	00	0
08	35	SUM	17	08	8	26	94	=

*Denotes 2nd function key

LOC	CODE	KEY	LOC	CODE	KEY	LOC	CODE	KEY
27	59	*pause	46	32	$x \leq t$	65	00	0
28	59	*pause	47	22	GTO	66	94	=
29	59	*pause	48	02	2	67	33	STO
30	35	SUM	49	03	3	68	07	7
31	00	0	50	33	STO	69	29	*Int
32	34	RCL	51	07	7	70	39	*EXC
33	00	0	52	29	*Int	71	07	7
34	56	*CP	53	64	×	72	12	INV
35	41	R/S	54	06	6	73	29	*Int
36	42	RST	55	00	0	74	54	÷
37	32	$x \leq t$	56	94	=	75	92	.
38	00	0	57	84	+	76	06	6
39	05	5	58	34	RCL	77	94	=
40	47	*$x \geq t$	59	07	7	78	35	SUM
41	04	4	60	12	INV	79	07	7
42	06	6	61	29	*Int	80	34	RCL
43	22	GTO	62	64	×	81	07	7
44	02	2	63	01	1	82	58	*rtn
45	03	3	64	00	0			

SR-56 SCORING PROGRAM II

*Scores one car at a time for up to six legs
at one point per hundredth of a minute early or late
(no maximum penalty)*

LOC	CODE	KEY	LOC	CODE	KEY	LOC	CODE	KEY
00	34	RCL	11	41	R/S	22	04	4
01	01	1	12	34	RCL	23	41	R/S
02	57	*subr	13	03	3	24	34	RCL
03	04	4	14	57	*subr	25	05	5
04	04	4	15	04	4	26	57	*subr
05	41	R/S	16	04	4	27	04	4
06	34	RCL	17	41	R/S	28	04	4
07	02	2	18	34	RCL	29	41	R/S
08	57	*subr	19	04	4	30	34	RCL
09	04	4	20	57	*subr	31	06	6
10	04	4	21	04	4	32	57	*subr

*Denotes 2nd function key

LOC	CODE	KEY	LOC	CODE	KEY	LOC	CODE	KEY
33	04	4	51	09	9	69	33	STO
34	04	4	52	35	SUM	70	07	7
35	34	RCL	53	08	8	71	29	*Int
36	00	0	54	34	RCL	72	64	×
37	64	×	55	09	9	73	06	6
38	01	1	56	57	*subr	74	00	0
39	00	0	57	06	6	75	94	=
40	00	0	58	09	9	76	84	+
41	94	=	59	74	−	77	34	RCL
42	41	R/S	60	34	RCL	78	07	7
43	42	RST	61	08	8	79	12	INV
44	57	*subr	62	94	=	80	29	*Int
45	06	6	63	59	*pause	81	64	×
46	09	9	64	59	*pause	82	01	1
47	39	*EXC	65	28	$*\|x\|$	83	00	0
48	08	8	66	35	SUM	84	00	0
49	57	*subr	67	00	0	85	94	=
50	06	6	68	58	*rtn	86	58	*rtn

SR-56 SCORING PROGRAM IIA

*Scores one car at a time for up to six legs
at one point per hundredth of a minute early or late,
with a maximum penalty for lateness*

LOC	CODE	KEY	LOC	CODE	KEY	LOC	CODE	KEY
00	57	*subr	12	57	*subr	24	01	1
01	05	5	13	05	5	25	00	0
02	00	0	14	00	0	26	00	0
03	39	*EXC	15	74	−	27	94	=
04	08	8	16	34	RCL	28	59	*pause
05	57	*subr	17	08	8	29	59	*pause
06	05	5	18	94	=	30	35	SUM
07	00	0	19	47	$*x \geq t$	31	00	0
08	35	SUM	20	03	3	32	34	RCL
09	08	8	21	07	7	33	00	0
10	34	RCL	22	93	+/−	34	56	*CP
11	09	9	23	64	×	35	41	R/S

*Denotes 2nd function key

LOC	CODE	KEY	LOC	CODE	KEY	LOC	CODE	KEY
36	42	RST	47	22	GTO	58	34	RCL
37	32	x ≤ t	48	02	2	59	07	7
38	00	0	49	03	3	60	12	INV
39	05	5	50	33	STO	61	29	*Int
40	47	*x ≥ t	51	07	7	62	64	×
41	04	4	52	29	*Int	63	01	1
42	06	6	53	64	×	64	00	0
43	22	GTO	54	06	6	65	00	0
44	02	2	55	00	0	66	94	=
45	03	3	56	94	=	67	58	*rtn
46	32	x ≤ t	57	84	+			

How Scoring Programs I and II work

Steps 00 – 01 recall the allowed time for leg 1. Steps 02 – 04 send the calculator to the first subroutine, which in turn sends it to a sub-subroutine. This sub-subroutine converts the allowed time to decimal minutes—minutes and hundredths—and sends the calculator back to the subroutine. Now the starting time is converted to decimal minutes and is added to the converted allowed time. This done, the finishing time is converted, and from it is subtracted the total of the allowed time and the starting time. The difference is the time error in decimal minutes. Program I multiplies the absolute value of the error (step 65) by 60 to give the point-per-second penalty; Program II multiplies by 100 to give the point-per-1/100-minute penalty.

When leg 1 has been scored, the calculator goes to step 05 and stops. As soon as you have stored the leg 2 start and finish times in R_8 and R_9, press R/S. The calculator now scores leg 2. And so on until the last leg has been scored. At this stage the accumulated point penalty is retrieved from R_0 and is displayed, and the calculator is ready to score the next car as soon as R_0 has been cleared.

Scoring with Programs I and II

Program I: Store allowed leg times in $R_1 - R_6$ as hours, decimal point, minutes, seconds. (For example, an allowed time for leg 1 of 1 hr. 2 min. 40 sec. is stored as 1.024 STO 1.)

Program II: Store allowed leg times in $R_1 - R_6$ as hours, decimal point, hundredths of minutes. (For example, an allowed time for leg 1 of 1 hr. 2.67 min. is stored as 1.0267 STO 1.)

Both programs: Using the same time notation, store Car 1's leg 1 starting time in R_8 and its leg 1 finishing time in R_9. Press RST R/S.

The calculator will pause at steps 62 − 64 and display the car's leg 1 error or penalty points (with a minus sign if the car was early) long enough—about 1 1/2 seconds—to be copied down.

When the calculator stops, store the car's leg 2 starting and finishing times in R_8 and R_9, respectively. Press R/S. (Do *not* press RST!) The calculator will again pause at steps 62 − 64 and display the leg 2 error or penalty. When it stops, store the car's leg 3 start and finish times and press R/S.

Continue until all six legs have been scored. At this point the calculator will display the car's total score for the six legs.

As soon as you have written down the total score, press 0 STO 0. The calculator is now ready to score Car 2. Simply store Car 2's leg 1 start finish times in R_8 and R_9 and proceed as before.

Important note: If there are fewer than six legs to be scored, the program will have to be modified slightly. Should there be only four legs, for instance, steps 23 − 25 must be changed to:

```
23   22   GTO
24   03    3
25   05    5
```

Should there be five legs, then steps 29 − 31 would be the ones to be changed to GTO 35. The intent here is of course to send the calculator from the last leg scoring calculations to the final summing-up procedure.

After the last leg has been scored, steps 25 − 37 of Program I (steps 35 − 42 of Program II) display the car's total penalty and stop the calculator, which is now ready to score the next car as soon as you have cleared R_0 by pressing 0 STO 0.

How Scoring Programs IA and IIA work

The subroutines each beginning at program step 50 convert the stored times to minutes and hundredths of minutes. In every case steps 00 – 02 start the conversion of the allowed time; steps 03 – 07 start the conversion of the starting time; steps 08 – 09 add the converted allowed and starting times in R_s. Steps 10 – 14 start the conversion of the finishing time; and steps 15 – 18 subtract the total of the allowed and starting times from the finishing time, producing at step 18 the time error if any.

Step 19, a conditional test controlling a program branch, asks whether the time error is equal to or greater than zero (R_t contains 0). If the answer is yes, the car was either on time or late, and the calculator goes to step 37. Steps 37 – 40 ask whether the car was less than 5 minutes late. If the answer is yes, steps 41 – 42, followed by steps 46 – 49 and 23 – 31, calculate the earned score and sum it into R_0. If the answer at step 40 is no, indicating that the car was at least 5 minutes late, steps 43 – 45 and then 23 – 31 calculate a 5-minute penalty and sum it into R_0.

Back at step 19, if the answer is no, meaning that the time error is negative (less than zero), the car was early. The program automatically skips to step 22, which changes the sign of the error from negative to positive. Then steps 23 – 31 calculate the earned score and sum it into R_0.

Step 34 clears R_t of any value that was placed in it at step 37. Steps 35 – 36 ready the calculator for the next scoring operation.

* * *

What about the time-conversion routines? In Program I (steps 69 – 98) and Program IA (steps 50 – 81), the hours-minutes-seconds time is converted in three stages. Assume a time of 1:23:45 (1 hr. 23 min. 45 sec.), which is keyed in as 1.2345.

The integer, 1 (hour), is multiplied by 60 to give 60 minutes.

The fraction, 0.2345, is multiplied by 100 to create the minutes-seconds expression 23.45. The integer, 23 (minutes), is added to the 60 minutes.

The fraction, 0.45 (representing 45 seconds), is divided by .6 to give .75 minute, which, added to 83, gives 83.75 minutes.

In Programs II (steps 69 – 85) and IIA (steps 50 – 66), the hours-minutes-decimal-minutes time is even easier to convert. Assume a time of 3 hrs. 45.67 minutes, which is keyed in as 3.4567.

The integer, 3 (hours), is multiplied by 60 to give 180 minutes. The fractional part, 0.4567, is multiplied by 100 to give 45.67 minutes. The two products added together total 225.67 minutes.

Scoring with Programs IA and IIA

Program IA; Store allowed leg times in $R_1 - R_6$ as hours, decimal point, minutes, seconds. (For example, an allowed leg 1 time of 58 min. 3 sec. is stored as .5803 STO 1.)

Program IIA: Store allowed leg times in $R_1 - R_6$ as hours, decimal point, minutes, hundredths of minutes. (For example, an allowed leg 1 time of 62.33 min. can be stored as either .6233 or 1.0233.)

Both programs: Programs steps 38 − 39 contain the maximum late penalty in whole minutes. As the program is printed here, the maximum is five minutes (300 points in Program IA, 500 points in Program IIA), but it can be as little as one minute (01) or as much as ninety-nine minutes (99).

Using the proper time notation from above, store Car 1's leg 1 starting time in R_8 and its leg 1 finishing time in R_9. Be sure that R_0 contains 0. Press RCL 1 RST R/S. The calculator figures the leg 1 penalty, displays it momentarily, then displays the total score so far and stops.

Store the leg 2 times in R_8 and R_9 and press RCL 2 R/S. The leg 2 penalty and the total score so far are displayed, and the calculator stops again.

Continue to score the remaining legs in the same manner. When the last leg has been scored and written down, press 0 STO 0. The calculator is ready to score Car 2.

(If there are fewer than six legs, nothing in these two programs needs to be changed.)

Checking Out the Scoring Programs

Before using any of these programs to score a real rally, practice all four routines and familiarize yourself with them thoroughly. For convenience in reading the display, *fix 4 is best, although for Program I *fix 0 serves very nicely. Remember that afternoon times must be expressed in 24-hour time. And keep in mind that the decimal point always goes between the hours and the minutes. If there are no hours to key in, the point precedes the minutes anyway; and if there are no minutes to key in, then point zero zero must precede the seconds or the hundredths of minutes.

---

*Denotes 2nd function key

To check out Programs I and IA you may wish to use these data:

Times in hours, minutes and seconds

	Allowed	Started	Finished
Leg 1	00:16:18	10:01:00	10:17:21
Leg 2	00:33:03	10:20:00	10:58:20
Leg 3	00:42:46	11:00:00	11:40:06
Leg 4	01:19:13	11:42:30	12:55:54
Leg 5	00:21:10	12:59:00	13:20:09
Leg 6	00:39:40	13:22:00	14:01:40

To verify Programs II and IIA use these figures:

Times in hours, minutes and hundredths

	Allowed	Started	Finished
Leg 1	00:16.30	10:01.00	10:17.35
Leg 2	00:33.05	10:20.00	10:58.33
Leg 3	00:42.77	11:00.00	11:40.01
Leg 4	01:19:22	11:42.50	12:55.83
Leg 5	00:21.16	12:59.00	13:20.17
Leg 6	00:39.67	13:22.00	14:01.67

Nota bene that the times printed here are in conventional rally scorecard notation. When you key them into the SR-56, a decimal point must invariably precede the minutes.

Your careful efforts should bring forth these results:

	Program I		Program IA		Program II		Program IIA	
Leg 1	3	3	3	3	0.05	0.05	5	5
Leg 2	317	317	300	303	5.28	5.28	50	505
Leg 3	− 160	160	160	463	− 2.76	2.76	276	781
Leg 4	− 349	349	349	812	− 5.93	5.89	589	1370
Leg 5	1	1	1	813	0.01	0.01	1	1371
Leg 6	0	0	0	813	0	0	0	1371
Total	830			813	1399			1371

SR-56 SCORING PROGRAM III

*Scores all cars checkpoint by checkpoint
at one point per hundredth of a minute error, with a
maximum penalty of five minutes (50 points)
early or late*

LOC	CODE	KEY	LOC	CODE	KEY	LOC	CODE	KEY
00	93	+/−	18	94	=	36	33	STO
01	57	*subr	19	59	*pause	37	09	9
02	03	3	20	59	*pause	38	29	*Int
03	06	6	21	28	$*\lvert x \rvert$	39	64	×
04	39	*EXC	22	47	$*x \geq t$	40	06	6
05	00	0	23	03	3	41	00	0
06	57	*subr	24	02	2	42	94	=
07	03	3	25	64	×	43	84	+
08	06	6	26	01	1	44	34	RCL
09	35	SUM	27	00	0	45	09	9
10	00	0	28	00	0	46	12	INV
11	05	5	29	94	=	47	29	*Int
12	32	$x \leq t$	30	41	R/S	48	64	×
13	34	RCL	31	42	RST	49	01	1
14	00	0	32	32	$x \leq t$	50	00	0
15	84	+	33	22	GTO	51	00	0
16	34	RCL	34	02	2	52	94	=
17	01	1	35	05	5	53	58	*rtn

Store the allowed time for leg 1 in R_1 as *minutes, decimal point, hundredths of minutes*. For example, an allowed time of 24.67 minutes is keyed in as 24.67 STO 1; a time of 1 hr. 5.09 minutes is keyed in as 65.09 STO 1.

To score the first car for leg 1, key in the car's time of leaving the start as *hours, decimal point, minutes and hundredths* and press STO 0; then key in the car's arrival time at the first checkpoint in the same way and press RST R/S.

The first display gives the time error in minutes and hundredths, preceded by a minus sign if the car was late. The second, final display shows the penalty points at 1 point per hundredth-minute error with a maximum of 500.

To score the second car for leg 1, key in the starting time, press STO 0; key in the finishing time and press R/S. When all the cars have been scored for leg 1, store the allowed time for leg 2 in R_1 and repeat the routine.

Appendix

Time-Speed-Distance Formulas

distance = speed × time speed = distance ÷ time

time = distance ÷ speed

miles = miles per hour × hours

$$\text{miles} = \frac{\text{miles per hour} \times \text{minutes}}{60}$$

$$\text{miles} = \frac{\text{miles per hour} \times \text{seconds}}{3600}$$

$$\text{miles per hour} = \frac{\text{miles}}{\text{hours}} \qquad \text{miles per hour} = \frac{\text{miles} \times 60}{\text{minutes}}$$

$$\text{miles per hour} = \frac{\text{miles} \times 3600}{\text{seconds}}$$

$$\text{miles per minute} = \frac{\text{miles}}{\text{hours} \times 60}$$

$$\text{feet per minute} = \frac{\text{miles per hour} \times 5280}{60}$$

$$\text{feet per second} = \frac{\text{miles per hour} \times 5280}{3600}$$

$$\text{hours} = \frac{\text{miles}}{\text{miles per hour}} \qquad \text{minutes} = \frac{\text{miles} \times 60}{\text{miles per hour}}$$

$$\text{seconds} = \frac{\text{miles} \times 3600}{\text{miles per hour}}$$

1 second = 0.016667 minute   0.01 minute = 0.6 second

$$\text{minutes per mile} = \frac{60}{\text{miles per hour}}$$

Correction Factors

$$\text{Factor A} = \frac{\text{official odometer check distance}}{\text{indicated odometer check distance}}$$

$$\text{Factor B} = \frac{\text{indicated odometer check distance}}{\text{official odometer check distance}}$$

official miles = odometer miles × Factor A
odometer miles = official miles × Factor B
indicated minutes per mile =
　　　　　　　　　　official minutes per mile × Factor A
indicated speed = official speed × Factor B

"Phantom Car" Formulas

Phantom car approaching

A = speed of phantom car in miles per hour
B = speed of rally car in miles per hour
C = miles between the two cars at the start
D = miles to be driven by rally car to meet phantom car
E = minutes to be driven by rally car to meet phantom car

$$A = \frac{B(C-D)}{D} \quad B = \frac{AD}{C-D} \quad C = \frac{D(A+B)}{B}$$

$$A = \frac{60C - BE}{E} \quad B = \frac{60C - AE}{E} \quad C = \frac{E(A+B)}{60}$$

$$D = \frac{BC}{A+B} \quad D = \frac{BE}{60} \quad E = \frac{60C}{A+B}$$

Phantom car going away

A = speed of phantom car in miles per hour
B = speed of rally car in miles per hour
C = miles phantom car is ahead at the start
D = miles to be driven by rally car to overtake phantom car
E = minutes phantom car is ahead at the start

$$A = \frac{B(D-C)}{D} \qquad B = \frac{AD}{D-C} \qquad C = \frac{D(B-A)}{B}$$

$$A = \frac{60BD}{60D + BE} \qquad B = \frac{60AD}{60D - AE} \qquad C = \frac{AE}{60}$$

$$D = \frac{BC}{B-A} \qquad D = \frac{ABE}{60(B-A)} \qquad E = \frac{60(B-A)}{AB}$$

HP-25 RALLY NAVIGATION PROGRAMS
HP-25 RALLY NAVIGATION PROGRAM I

Calculates allowed time as elapsed (stopwatch) time in minutes and hundredths of minutes

Keycodes			Keystrokes	Keycodes			Keystrokes
00				09		61	×
01		24	01	RCL 1	10	23	51	00	STO + 0
02			41	−	11		24	01	RCL 1
03	23	51	01	STO + 1	12		24	04	RCL 4
04		24	03	RCL 3	13			61	×
05		24	02	RCL 2	14		23	06	STO 6
06			71	÷	15		24	01	RCL 1
07		24	04	RCL 4	16		14	74	*f* PAUSE
08			61	×	17		24	00	RCL 0

(To display allowed times in minutes and seconds add: 18 14 00 *f* H.MS)

HP-25 RALLY NAVIGATION PROGRAM II

Calculates allowed time as clock time (time of day) in hours, minutes and seconds

Keycodes			Keystrokes	Keycodes			Keystrokes
00					07			71	÷
01	14	11	02	*f* FIX 2	08		24	04	RCL 4
02		24	01	RCL 1	09			61	×
03			41	−	10			61	×
04	23	51	01	STO + 1	11	23	51	00	STO + 0
05		24	03	RCL 3	12		24	03	RCL 3
06		24	02	RCL 2	13			71	÷

Keystrokes				Keycodes	Keycodes			Keystrokes
14	23	51	07	STO + 7	19		24 01	RCL 1
15		24	01	RCL 1	20		14 74	f PAUSE
16		24	04	RCL 4	21		24 07	RCL 7
17			61	×	22	14	11 04	f FIX 4
18		23	06	STO 6	23		14 00	f H.MS

HP-25 RALLY NAVIGATION PROGRAM III

Calculates allowed time as elapsed (stopwatch) time in minutes and hundredths of minutes and as clock time (time of day) in hours, minutes and seconds

Keycodes				Keystrokes	Keycodes				Keystrokes
00					13			71	÷
01	14	11	02	f FIX 2	14	23	51	07	STO + 7
02		24	01	RCL 1	15		24	01	RCL 1
03			41	−	16		24	04	RCL 4
04	23	51	01	STO + 1	17			61	×
05		24	03	RCL 3	18		23	06	STO 6
06		24	02	RCL 2	19		24	01	RCL 1
07			71	÷	20		14	74	f PAUSE
08		24	04	RCL 4	21		24	00	RCL 0
09			61	×	22		14	74	f PAUSE
10			61	×	23		24	07	RCL 7
11	23	51	00	STO + 0	24	14	11	04	f FIX 4
12		24	03	RCL 3	25		14	00	f H.MS

Data Entries

1. Average speed in miles per hour STO 2
2. 60 STO 3
3. Factor A:
    odometer check official distance in miles
    ENTER
    odometer check indicated distance in miles
    ÷ STO 4
4. Factor B:
    with Factor A still displayed—
    g 1/x STO 5

> *or*
> odometer check indicated distance in miles
> ENTER
> odometer check official distance in miles
> ÷ STO 5

5. *Programs II and III only:*
> starting time as hours, decimal point, minutes and seconds
> *g* H STO 7

Program Initialization

1. *f* PRGM
2. Key in distance in miles (or miles and hundredths) for which the allowed time is wanted
3. R/S
4. For subsequent time checks key in the odometer distance and press R/S

Callouts—

(between program runs)

1. RCL 0 displays accumulated allowed time in minutes and hundredths
2. RCL 1 displays last entered odometer distance
3. RCL 2 displays current average speed
4. RCL 3 displays the constant 60
5. RCL 4 displays Factor A
6. RCL 5 displays Factor B
7. RCL 6 displays the official-distance equivalent of the odometer distance stored in R_1
8. *Programs II and III only:*
   RCL 7 displays allowed time as clock time in decimal hours:
   RCL 7 *f* H.MS displays allowed time as clock time in hours, minutes and seconds

To Change Average Speed

1. Key in odometer reading at speed-change point
2. R/S
3. Key in new average speed
4. STO 2
5. Key in next odometer distance for which the allowed time is wanted
6. R/S

For the Odometer Equivalent of an Official Distance
    1. Key in the odometer distance in miles (or miles and hundredths)
    2. RCL 5 ×

Pause (Lose Time)

Key in the amount of time to be lost:
a. as minutes and hundredths
    (1) *Program I:* GTO 10 R/S
    (2) *Programs II and III:* GTO 11 R/S
b. as minutes and seconds
    (1) *Program I:* g H GTO 10 R/S
    (2) *Programs II and III:* g H GTO 11 R/S

Gain Time

Key in the amount of time to be gained:
a. as minutes and hundredths
    (1) *Program I:* CHS GTO 10 R/S
    (2) *Programs II and III:* CHS GTO 11 R/S
b. as minutes and seconds
    (1) *Program I:* CHS g H GTO 10 R/S
    (2) *Programs II and III:* CHS g H GTO 11 R/S

To Correct Allowed Time for Off-Course Distance

1. Calculate total off-course distance:	
Odometer reading at turnaround	ENTER
Odometer reading at return to point of original error	−
2.	2 ×
3. If Program I is in use	*GTO 04 R/S
If Program II or III is in use	*GTO 05 R/S

Procedure at the End of a Leg
    1. 0 STO 0 STO 1 (clears R_0 and R_1)
    2. If there is a new average speed, key it in and press STO 2
    3. *If Program II or Program III is in use—*
        starting time as hours, decimal point, minutes and seconds
        g H STO 7

---

*Because the higher odometer reading is subtracted from the lower one in step 1, step 2 gives the *negative* value of the total off-course distance; therefore it is not necessary to change the sign as was done in the example in Chapter 6.

4. Key in the distance in miles (or miles and hundredths) for which the allowed time is wanted
5. R/S

HP-25 RALLY NAVIGATION PROGRAM I
MODIFIED FOR TIME-BASED ROUTE INSTRUCTIONS

Calculates the allowed running time as elapsed time and calculates the time-based distance

Keycodes			Keystrokes	Keycodes			Keystrokes
00				16	14	74	f PAUSE
01		24	01 RCL 1	17	24	00	RCL 0
02			41 −	18*	15	74	g NOP
03	23	51	01 STO + 1	19	13	00	GTO 00
04		24	03 RCL 3	20	24	07	RCL 7
05		24	02 RCL 2	21	24	00	RCL 0
06			71 ÷	22		41	−
07		24	04 RCL 4	23	24	02	RCL 2
08			61 ×	24		61	×
09			61 ×	25	24	03	RCL 3
10	23	51	00 STO + 0	26		71	÷
11		24	01 RCL 1	27	24	05	RCL 5
12		24	04 RCL 4	28		61	×
13			61 ×	29	24	01	RCL 1
14		23	06 STO 6	30		51	+
15		24	01 RCL 1				

Data entries, program initialization, callouts, etc., are all exactly the same as for unmodified Program I with these additions:

Data Entry

Store the time-base time in R_7 either as:

    minutes, decimal point, hundredths STO 7

or as:

    minutes, decimal point, seconds *g* H STO 7

Callouts

    RCL 7 displays the time-based time as minutes and hundredths

---

*To display allowed running times as minutes and seconds rather than minutes and hundredths, key in step 18 as *f* H.MS.

Operation

To obtain the current time-based distance, press GTO 20 R/S

SR-56 RALLY NAVIGATION PROGRAMS

SR-56 RALLY NAVIGATION PROGRAM I

Calculates allowed time as elapsed (stopwatch) time in minutes and hundredths of minutes

LOC	CODE	KEY	LOC	CODE	KEY
00	74	–	16	35	SUM
01	34	RCL	17	00	0
02	01	1	18	34	RCL
03	94	=	19	01	1
04	35	SUM	20	59	*pause
05	01	1	21	59	*pause
06	64	×	22	64	×
07	34	RCL	23	34	RCL
08	03	3	24	04	4
09	54	÷	25	94	=
10	34	RCL	26	33	STO
11	02	2	27	06	6
12	64	×	28	34	RCL
13	34	RCL	29	00	0
14	04	4	30	41	R/S
15	94	=	31	42	RST

SR-56 RALLY NAVIGATION PROGRAM IA

Calculates allowed time as elapsed (stopwatch) time in minutes and hundredths of minutes and in minutes and seconds

LOC	CODE	KEY	LOC	CODE	KEY
00	74	–	04	35	SUM
01	34	RCL	05	01	1
02	01	1	06	64	×
03	94	=	07	34	RCL

---

*Denotes 2nd function key   (continued on page 198)

LOC	CODE	KEY	LOC	CODE	KEY
08	03	3	29	00	0
09	54	÷	30	59	*pause
10	34	RCL	31	59	*pause
11	02	2	32	33	STO
12	64	×	33	09	9
13	34	RCL	34	12	INV
14	04	4	35	29	*Int
15	94	=	36	64	×
16	35	SUM	37	92	.
17	00	0	38	06	6
18	34	RCL	39	94	=
19	01	1	40	39	*EXC
20	59	*pause	41	09	9
21	59	*pause	42	29	*Int
22	64	×	43	84	+
23	34	RCL	44	34	RCL
24	04	4	45	09	9
25	94	=	46	94	=
26	33	STO	47	41	R/S
27	06	6	48	42	RST
28	34	RCL			

SR-56 Navigation Programs I and IA

Data Entries

1. Average speed in miles per hour STO 2
2. 60 STO 3
3. Factor A:
   official length of odometer check ÷ odometer reading at end of odometer check STO 4
4. Factor B:
   with Factor A still displayed, press: *1/x STO 5

Program Initialization

1. Key in distance in miles for which the allowed time is wanted

---

*Denotes 2nd function key

2. RST *fix 2
3. R/S
4. For subsequent time checks key in the distance and press R/S

To Change Average Speed

1. Key in the odometer reading at the speed-change point
2. R/S
3. Key in the new average speed
4. STO 2
5. Key in the next odometer distance for which the allowed time is wanted
6. R/S

For the Odometer Equivalent of an Official Distance

1. Key in the official distance
2. Press × RCL 5=

Pause (Lose Time)

1. Key in the amount of time to be lost *in minutes and hundredths* (to convert seconds to hundredths of minutes, divide the seconds by 60)
2. Press GTO 16 R/S

Gain Time

1. Key in the amount of time to be gained *in minutes and hundredths*
2. Press +/− GTO 16 R/S

To Correct Allowed Time for Off-Course Distance

1. Key in odometer reading at turnaround
2. Press − (subtract)
3. Key in odometer reading at return to point of original error
4. Press = × 2 = GTO 06 R/S

Procedure at End of Leg

1. Press 0 STO 0 STO 1
2. If there is a new average speed, store it in R_2
3. Key in the first odometer distance for which the allowed time is wanted and press R/S

---

*Denotes 2nd function key

Time Displays After One Hour

Allowed times of one hour or more will be displayed in minutes

Callouts

Between program runs—

RCL 0 displays accumulated allowed time
RCL 1 displays last entered odometer distance
RCL 2 displays the average speed in use
RCL 3 displays the constant 60
RCL 4 displays Factor A
RCL 5 displays Factor B
RCL 6 displays the official-distance equivalent of the distance stored in R_1

SR-56 SUPPLEMENTARY ROUTINE FOR TIME-BASED INSTRUCTIONS

Calculates the odometer reading at which a time-identified action point will be found

(For use in conjunction with SR-56 Navigation Program I or IA only)

LOC	CODE	KEY	LOC	CODE	KEY
51	52	(	63	34	RCL
52	34	RCL	64	03	3
53	07	7	65	64	×
54	74	−	66	34	RCL
55	34	RCL	67	05	5
56	00	0	68	53	)
57	53	)	69	84	+
58	64	×	70	34	RCL
59	52	(	71	01	1
60	34	RCL	72	94	=
61	02	2	73	41	R/S
62	54	÷	74	42	RST

Data Entry

Key in the time-base time as minutes, decimal point, hundredths of minutes and press STO 7

Program Supplement Use

Before *and* after every speed change, pause and gain press GTO 51 R/S to display the latest calculable time-based distance

SR-56 RALLY NAVIGATION PROGRAM II

Calculates allowed time as clock time (time of day) in hours, minutes and seconds

LOC	CODE	KEY	LOC	CODE	KEY	LOC	CODE	KEY
00	74	−	29	53	)	58	94	=
01	34	RCL	30	33	STO	59	33	STO
02	01	1	31	09	9	60	06	6
03	94	=	32	29	*Int	61	34	RCL
04	35	SUM	33	64	×	62	00	0
05	01	1	34	92	.	63	41	R/S
06	54	÷	35	00	0	64	42	RST
07	34	RCL	36	01	1	65	33	STO
08	02	2	37	53	)	66	09	9
09	64	×	38	84	+	67	29	*Int
10	34	RCL	39	52	(	68	84	+
11	04	4	40	34	RCL	69	52	(
12	94	=	41	09	9	70	34	RCL
13	35	SUM	42	12	INV	71	09	9
14	03	3	43	29	*Int	72	12	INV
15	34	RCL	44	64	×	73	29	*Int
16	03	3	45	92	.	74	64	×
17	33	STO	46	00	0	75	01	1
18	09	9	47	00	0	76	00	0
19	29	*Int	48	06	6	77	00	0
20	84	+	49	94	=	78	53	)
21	52	(	50	33	STO	79	33	STO
22	34	RCL	51	00	0	80	09	9
23	09	9	52	34	RCL	81	29	*Int
24	12	INV	53	01	1	82	54	÷
25	29	*Int	54	59	*pause	83	06	6
26	64	×	55	64	×	84	00	0
27	06	6	56	34	RCL	85	53	)
28	00	0	57	04	4	86	84	+

*Denotes 2nd function key

LOC	CODE	KEY	LOC	CODE	KEY	LOC	CODE	KEY
87	52	(	91	29	*Int	96	35	SUM
88	34	RCL	92	54	÷	97	03	3
89	09	9	93	03	3	98	41	R/S
90	12	INV	94	06	6	99	42	RST
			95	94	=			

SR-56 RALLY NAVIGATION PROGRAM IIA

Calculates allowed time as clock time (time of day) in hours, minutes and hundredths of minutes

LOC	CODE	KEY	LOC	CODE	KEY	LOC	CODE	KEY
00	74	−	22	12	INV	44	34	RCL
01	34	RCL	23	29	*Int	45	00	0
02	01	1	24	64	×	46	49	*fix
03	94	=	25	92	.	47	04	4
04	35	SUM	26	06	6	48	41	R/S
05	01	1	27	84	+	49	42	RST
06	54	÷	28	34	RCL	50	33	STO
07	34	RCL	29	09	9	51	09	9
08	02	2	30	94	=	52	29	*Int
09	64	×	31	33	STO	53	39	*EXC
10	34	RCL	32	00	0	54	09	9
11	04	4	33	34	RCL	55	12	INV
12	94	=	34	04	4	56	29	*Int
13	35	SUM	35	64	×	57	54	÷
14	03	3	36	34	RCL	58	92	.
15	34	RCL	37	01	1	59	06	6
16	03	3	38	49	*fix	60	84	+
17	33	STO	39	02	2	61	34	RCL
18	09	9	40	59	*pause	62	09	9
19	20	*Int	41	94	=	63	22	GTO
20	39	*EXC	42	33	STO	64	01	1
21	09	9	43	06	6	65	02	2

SR-56 Average-Speed Navigation Programs II and IIA
Data Entries

1. Average speed in miles per hour STO 2
2. *Program II* — Key in assigned starting time of day as hours,

---

*Denotes 2nd function key

decimal point, minutes and seconds (if any) and press GTO 65 R/S (then press GTO 15 R/S if you wish)

Program IIA—Key in assigned starting time of day as hours, decimal point, minutes and hundredths (if any) and press GTO 50 R/S

3. Factor A:
   official length of odometer check ÷
   odometer reading at end of check STO 4
   Factor B:
   with Factor A still displayed:
   *1/x STO 5

Program Initialization

1. Key in distance for which the allowed time is wanted
2. *fix 4 RST
3. R/S
4. For subsequent time checks key in the distance and press R/S

To Change Average Speed

1. Key in the odometer reading at the speed-change point
2. R/S
3. Key in the new average speed
4. STO 2
5. Key in the next odometer distance for which the allowed time is wanted
6. R/S

For the Odometer Equivalent of an Official Distance

1. Key in the official distance
2. Press × RCL 5 =

Pauses (Lose Time) and Gains

Program II—If the length of the pause or gain is given in minutes and seconds, key it in as decimal point, minutes and seconds and press GTO 65 R/S for a pause, +/− GTO 65 R/S for a gain

If the length of the pause or gain is given in minutes and hundredths, convert the hundredths of minutes to seconds and key in the time as decimal point, minutes and seconds (to convert

---

*Denotes 2nd function key

hundredths of minutes to seconds, multiply the hundredths by 0.6; then add the whole minutes, and finally divide the answer by 100; for example, 2.5 minutes is treated as .5 × .6 + 2 = ÷ 100 = (result: 0.023) and press GTO 65 R/S for a pause, +/− GTO 65 R/S for a gain

Program IIA—If the length of the pause or gain is given in minutes and seconds, key it in as decimal point, minutes and hundredths (to convert seconds to hundredths, divide the hundredths by 60; then add the whole minutes, and finally divide the answer by 100; for example, 2 min. 45 sec. is keyed in as 45 ÷ 60 = + 2 = ÷ 100 = (result: 0.0275) and press GTO 50 R/S for a pause, +/− GTO 50 R/S for a gain

If the length of the pause or gain is given in minutes and hundredths, key it in as decimal point, minutes and hundredths and press GTO 50 R/S for a pause, + / − GTO 50 R/S for a gain

To Correct Allowed Time for Off-Course Distance
1. Key in odometer reading at turnaround
2. Press − (subtract)
3. Key in odometer reading at return to point of original error
4. Press = × 2 = GTO 06 R/S

Procedure at End of Leg
1. Press 0 STO 0 STO 1 STO 3
2. If there is a new average speed, store it in R_2
3. *Program II*—Key in assigned time of starting the next leg as hours, decimal point, minutes and seconds (if any) and press GTO 65 R/S (then GTO 15 R/S if you wish)
   Program IIA—Key in assigned time of starting the next leg as hours, decimal point, minutes and hundredths (if any) and press GTO 50 R/S

Callouts
　　Between program runs—
　　RCL 0 displays the allowed time:
　　　　Program II: as hours, decimal point, minutes, seconds
　　　　Program IIA: as hours, decimal point, minutes, hundredths

RCL 1 displays the latest-entered odometer distance
RCL 2 displays the average speed in use
RCL 3 displays the latest allowed time in decimal hours
RCL 4 displays Factor A
RCL 5 displays Factor B
RCL 6 displays the official-distance equivalent of the odometer distance in R_1.

HP-25 SCORING PROGRAMS
HP-25 SCORING PROGRAM I

*Scores one car at a time for up to seven legs
at one point per second early or late
(no maximum penalty)*

Keycodes			Keystrokes	Keycodes			Keystrokes
00							
01		32	CHS	11		03	3
02	15	00	gH	12		06	6
03		21	$x \leq y$	13		00	0
04	15	00	g H	14		00	0
05		51	+	15		61	×
06		21	$x \leq y$	16	14	74	f PAUSE
07	15	00	g H	17	14	74	f PAUSE
08		51	+	18	15	03	g ABS
09	14	00	f H.MS	19	23 51	00	STO + 0
10	15	00	g H	20		13 00	GTO 00

HP-25 Scoring Program I

Data Entries

1. Key in allowed time for Leg 1 as hours, decimal point, minutes and seconds and press STO 1
2. Key in allowed time for Leg 2 and press STO 2
3. Key in allowed times for Leg 3 up to Leg 7 similarly

Program Initialization

1. *f* PRM
2. *f* FIX 0
3. RCL 1
4. Key in car's starting time for Leg 1 as hours, decimal point, minutes and seconds

5. ENTER
6. Key in car's finishing time for Leg 1 as hours, decimal point, minutes and seconds
7. R/S
8. When the program run ends and the Leg 1 score is displayed, press RCL 2
9. Key in car's starting time for Leg 2 as hours, decimal point, minutes and seconds
10. ENTER
11. Key in car's finishing time for Leg 2 as hours, decimal point, minutes and seconds
12. R/S
13. Repeat this procedure for up to seven legs
14. When the program has been run for the final leg, press RCL 0 to display the car's total point score
15. 0 STO 0 (R_0 *must* be cleared before next car is scored)
16. Score the next car in the same way, starting at program initialization procedure 3 above

Displays

First display gives time error in seconds (preceded by a minus sign if the car was late)

Second display gives the point score (always positive) for the leg just scored

Callouts

Between program runs:

RCL 0 displays car's current accumulated score
RCL 1 . . . RCL 7 displays the stored allowed times for Legs 1 – 7

HP-25 MAXIMUM-PENALTY SCORING PROGRAM IA

Scores one car at a time for up to seven legs at one point per second early or late with a maximum penalty for lateness of 5 minutes or 300 points

Keycodes		Keystrokes	Keycodes		Keystrokes
00					
01		32 CHS	03		21 $x \leq y$
02	15	00 *g* H	04	15	00 *g* H

Keycodes			Keystrokes	Keycodes			Keystrokes
05		51	+	20	15	51	$g\ x \geq 0$
06		21	$x \leq y$	21	13	33	GTO 33
07	15	00	g H	22	14	73	f LASTx
08		51	+	23		03	3
09	14	00	f H.MS	24		06	6
10	15	00	g H	25		00	0
11	15	51	$g\ x \geq 0$	26		00	0
12	13	23	GTO 23	27		61	×
13		31	ENTER	28	14	74	f PAUSE
14		31	ENTER	29	14	74	f PAUSE
15		73	•	30	15	03	g ABS
16		00	0	31	23 51	00	STO + 0
17		05	5	32	13	00	GTO 00
18	15	00	g H	33		22	R↓
19		51	+	34	13	23	GTO 23

HP-25 Maximum-Penalty Scoring Program IA

Alternate Program Entries for Maximum Late Time Steps 16 and 17

> Where maximum late time is other than 5 minutes:
> if time is 6 minutes, key in (16) 0, (17) 6
> if time is 10 minutes, key in (16) 1, (17) 0
> if time is 15 minutes, key in (16) 1, (17) 5

Data Entries

> Same as for the Scoring Program I

Program Initialization

> Same as for the Scoring Program I

Callouts

> Same as for the Scoring Program I

HP-25 HOURS AND DECIMAL MINUTES SCORING PROGRAM II

Scores one car at a time for up to six legs at one point per hundredth of a minute early or late with no maximal penalty

Keycodes			Keystrokes	Keycodes			Keystrokes
00				17		61	×
01		22	R↓	18	23	51 00	STO + 0
02		22	R↓	19		15 41	g x < 0
03	23	00	STO 0	20		13 32	GTO 32
04		22	R↓	21		24 00	RCL 0
05		22	R↓	22	14	11 02	f FIX 2
06		32	CHS	23		14 74	f PAUSE
07		31	ENTER	24		14 74	f PAUSE
08	15	01	g FRAC	25		15 03	g ABS
09		33	EEX	26		33	EEX
10		02	2	27		02	2
11		61	×	28		61	×
12	23	51 00	STO + 0	29	23	51 07	STO + 7
13		22	R↓	30	14	11 00	f FIX 0
14	14	01	f INT	31		13 00	GTO 00
15		06	6	32		22	R↓
16		00	0	33		13 08	GTO 08

HP-25 MAXIMUM-PENALTY SCORING PROGRAM IIA

*Scores one car at a time for up to six legs
at one point per hundredth of a minute early or late
with a maximum penalty for lateness of 5 minutes or 500 points*

Keycodes			Keystrokes	Keycodes			Keystrokes
00				15		06	6
01		22	R↓	16		00	0
02		22	R↓	17		61	×
03	23	00	STO 0	18	23	51 00	STO + 0
04		22	R↓	19		15 41	g x < 0
05		22	R↓	20		13 34	GTO 34
06		32	CHS	21		24 00	RCL 0
07		31	ENTER	22	14	11 02	f FIX 2
08	15	01	g FRAC	23		14 74	f PAUSE
09		33	EEX	24		14 74	f PAUSE
10		02	2	25		15 41	g x < 0
11		61	×	26		13 36	GTO 36
12	23	51 00	STO + 0	27		33	EEX
13		22	R↓	28		02	2
14	14	01	f INT				

Keycodes		Keystrokes		Keycodes		Keystrokes
29			61 ×	38		00	0
30		15	03 g ABS	39		05	5
31	23	51	07 STO + 7	40		51	+
32	14	11	00 f FIX 0	41	15	51	$g\ x \geq 0$
33		13	00 GTO 00	42	13	45	GTO 45
34			22 R↓	43	14	73	f LASTx
35		13	07 GTO 07	44	13	27	GTO 27
36			31 ENTER	45		22	R↓
37			31 ENTER	46	13	27	GTO 27

HP-25 Scoring Program II (no maximum)
and Scoring Program IIA (maximum late penalty)

Data Entries

1. Key in allowed time for Leg 1 as minutes, decimal point, hundredths of minutes
2. STO 1
3. Key in allowed time for Legs 2, 3, 4, 5 and 6 in the same way, following the respective time entries with STO 2, STO 3, STO 4, STO 5, STO 6

Alternate Program Entries for Maximum Late Time
(Steps 38 and 39, Program IIA)

Where maximum late time is other than 5 minutes:
   if time is 6 minutes, key in (38) *g* NOP or (38) 0, (39) 6
   if time is 10 minutes, key in (38) 1, (39) 0
   if time is 15 minutes, key in (38) 1, (39) 5

Program Initialization

1. *f* PRGM
2. RCL 1
3. Key in Car 1's starting time for Leg 1 as hours, decimal point, minutes and hundredths
4. ENTER
5. Key in Car 1's finishing time for Leg 1 as hours, decimal point, minutes and hundredths
6. R/S
7. RCL 2
8. Key in Car 1's starting time for Leg 2
9. ENTER

10. Key in Car 1's finishing time for Leg 2
11. R/S
12. Continue this procedure for as many as six legs.
13. When the last leg has been scored, RCL 7 will display the car's total score; record the score
14. 0 STO 7; the calculator is now ready to score Car 2 starting at program initialization procedure 2

Callouts

Between program runs:

RCL 1 . . . RCL 6 displays the stored allowed times for Legs 1 – 6

RCL 7 displays the car's current accumulated point score

HP-25 CHECKPOINT BY CHECKPOINT SCORING PROGRAM III

Scores one leg at a time at one point per hundredth of a minute early or late with a flat maximum penalty of 5 minutes or 500 points

Keycodes			Keystrokes	Keycodes			Keystrokes
00				21	14	74	*f* PAUSE
01		32	CHS	22	15	03	*g* ABS
02		31	ENTER	23		31	ENTER
03	15	01	*g* FRAC	24		31	ENTER
04		33	EEX	25		05	5
05		02	2	26		41	–
06		61	×	27	15	41	*g* x < 0
07	23	51 00	STO + 0	28	13	38	GTO 38
08		22	R↓	29	14	73	*f* LASTx
09	14	01	*f* INT	30		33	EEX
10		06	6	31		02	2
11		00	0	32		61	×
12		61	×	33		00	0
13	23	51 00	STO + 0	34	23	00	STO 0
14	15	41	*g* x < 0	35		22	R↓
15	13	40	GTO 40	36	14	11 00	*f* FIX 0
16	24	00	RCL 0	37	13	00	GTO 00
17	24	01	RCL 1	38		22	R↓
18		51	+	39	13	30	GTO 30
19	14	11 02	*f* FIX 2	40		22	R↓
20	14	11 02	*f* PAUSE	41	13	02	GTO 02

HP-25 Scoring Program III

Data Entry

Key in allowed time for Leg 1 as minutes, decimal point, hundredths of minutes

STO 1

Program Initialization

1. f PRGM
2. Key in car's starting time as hours, decimal point, minutes and hundredths
3. ENTER
4. Key in car's finishing time in the same way
5. R/S
6. To score the next car, go back to initialization step 2
7. To score the next leg, store the allowed time in R_1 and proceed to initialization step 2

Displays

1. Time error in minutes and hundredths (negative if late)
2. Point score

Callouts

Between program runs, RCL 1 f FIX 2 verifies allowed time for leg being scored

SR-56 SCORING PROGRAM I
SR-56 Scoring Programs

Scores one car at a time for up to six legs
at one point per second early or late
(no maximum penalty)

LOC	CODE	KEY	LOC	CODE	KEY	LOC	CODE	KEY
00	34	RCL	04	09	9	08	57	*subr
01	01	1	05	41	R/S	09	03	3
02	57	*subr	06	34	RCL	10	09	9
03	03	3	07	02	2	11	41	R/S

*Denotes 2nd function key

LOC	CODE	KEY	LOC	CODE	KEY	LOC	CODE	KEY
12	34	RCL	41	09	9	71	29	*Int
13	03	3	42	39	*EXC	72	64	×
14	57	*subr	43	08	8	73	06	6
15	03	3	44	57	*subr	74	00	0
16	09	9	45	06	6	75	84	+
17	41	R/S	46	09	9	76	52	(
18	34	RCL	47	35	SUM	77	34	RCL
19	04	4	48	08	8	78	07	7
20	57	*subr	49	34	RCL	79	12	INV
21	03	3	50	09	9	80	29	*Int
22	09	9	51	57	*subr	81	64	×
23	41	R/S	52	06	6	82	01	1
24	34	RCL	53	09	9	83	00	0
25	05	5	54	74	−	84	00	0
26	57	*subr	55	34	RCL	85	53	)
27	03	3	56	08	8	86	33	STO
28	09	9	57	94	=	87	07	7
29	41	R/S	58	64	×	88	29	*Int
30	34	RCL	59	06	6	89	84	+
31	06	6	60	00	0	90	52	(
32	57	*subr	61	94	=	91	34	RCL
33	03	3	62	59	*pause	92	07	7
34	09	9	63	59	*pause	93	12	INV
35	34	RCL	64	59	*pause	94	29	*Int
36	00	0	65	28	*|x|	95	54	÷
37	41	R/S	66	35	SUM	96	92	•
38	42	RST	67	00	0	97	06	6
39	57	*subr	68	58	*rtn	98	94	=
40	06	6	69	33	STO	99	58	*rtn
			70	07	7			

SR-56 Scoring Program I

Program Note

If there are fewer than six rally legs to be scored, the program must be modified. To avoid confusion, we suggest that you store the program exactly as it is printed and then adjust it in this way:

---

*Denotes 2nd function key

Number of legs to be scored	In execute mode, press:
5	GTO 29 LRN GTO 35 LRN RST
4	GTO 23 LRN GTO 35 LRN RST
3	GTO 17 LRN GTO 35 LRN RST
2	GTO 11 LRN GTO 35 LRN RST

Data Entries

Key in the allowed leg times as hours, decimal point, minutes, seconds:

Leg 1	STO 1	Leg 4	STO 4
Leg 2	STO 2	Leg 5	STO 5
Leg 3	STO 3	Leg 6	STO 6

Program Execution

Key in Car 1's leg 1 starting time as hours, decimal point, minutes, seconds and press STO 8; key in Car 1's leg 1 finishing time in the same units and press STO 9; press *fix 0 RST R/S.

The pause at steps 62 − 64 displays the penalty (with a minus sign if the car was early).

When the program has run, key in Car 1's leg 2 starting time STO 8 and its leg 2 finishing time STO 9 R/S (do *not* press RST!).

Repeat the procedure until Car 1's last leg has been scored. The display is then Car 1's total penalty for these legs.

Press 0 STO 0; R_0 now *must* be cleared.

Proceed to score Car 2 in the same fashion.

SR-56 SCORING PROGRAM IA

Scores one car at a time for up to six legs at one point per second early or late, with a maximum penalty for lateness

LOC	CODE	KEY	LOC	CODE	KEY	LOC	CODE	KEY
00	57	*subr	04	08	8	08	35	SUM
01	05	5	05	57	*subr	09	08	8
02	00	0	06	05	5	10	34	RCL
03	39	*EXC	07	00	0	11	09	9

*Denotes 2nd function key

LOC	CODE	KEY	LOC	CODE	KEY	LOC	CODE	KEY
12	57	*subr	36	42	RST	60	12	INV
13	05	5	37	32	$x \leq t$	61	29	*Int
14	00	0	38	00	0	62	64	×
15	74	−	39	05	5	63	01	1
16	34	RCL	40	47	*$x \geq t$	64	00	0
17	08	8	41	04	4	65	00	0
18	94	=	42	06	6	66	94	=
19	47	*$x \geq t$	43	22	GTO	67	33	STO
20	03	3	44	02	2	68	07	7
21	07	7	45	03	3	69	29	*Int
22	93	+/−	46	32	$x \leq t$	70	39	*EXC
23	64	×	47	22	GTO	71	07	7
24	06	6	48	02	2	72	12	INV
25	00	0	49	03	3	73	29	*Int
26	94	=	50	33	STO	74	54	÷
27	59	*pause	51	07	7	75	92	•
28	59	*pause	52	29	*Int	76	06	6
29	59	*pause	53	64	×	77	94	=
30	35	SUM	54	06	6	78	35	SUM
31	00	0	55	00	0	79	07	7
32	34	RCL	56	94	=	80	34	RCL
33	00	0	57	84	+	81	07	7
34	56	*CP	58	34	RCL	82	58	*rtn
35	41	R/S	59	07	7			

SR-56 Scoring Program IA

Program Notes

Locations 38-39 store in program memory the maximum late time in whole minutes. As the program is printed here, the max is 05 minutes. It can of course be any number of minutes from 01 to 99. Observe, however, that if there is no maximum, you cannot key in 0 and 0 at steps 38-39. You could store 99 minutes, which would probably be effective enough. But it would be better to make use of Program I, which, since it includes no tests for maximum lateness, is able to advance the calculator automatically to the next leg to be scored.

---

*Denotes 2nd function key

If there are fewer than six legs to be scored, nothing in the program needs to be changed. The display at the end of each program run always gives the car's accumulated point score.

Data Entries

Key in the allowed leg times as hours, decimal point, minutes and seconds:

Leg 1	STO 1	Leg 4	STO 4
Leg 2	STO 2	Leg 5	STO 5
Leg 3	STO 3	Leg 6	STO 6

Program Execution

Key in Car 1's leg 1 starting time as hours, decimal point, minutes, seconds and press STO 8; key in Car 1's leg 1 finishing time in the same units and press STO 9.

Now press RST RCL 1 R/S. The first display (steps 27 − 29) shows the leg 1 penalty. The display at step 35 shows the accumulated penalty.

Key in Car 1's leg 2 starting time STO 8, and the finishing time STO 9.

Press RCL 2 R/S. The first display shows the leg 2 penalty. The display at step 35 shows the accumulated penalty.

Score the remaining legs in the same way. When the last leg has been scored and the total penalty points have been recorded, press 0 STO 0. The calculator is now ready to score Car 2.

SR-56 SCORING PROGRAM II

Scores one car at a time for up to six legs at one point per hundredth of a minute early or late (no maximum penalty)

LOC	CODE	KEY	LOC	CODE	KEY	LOC	CODE	KEY
00	34	RCL	04	04	4	08	57	*subr
01	01	1	05	41	R/S	09	04	4
02	57	*subr	06	34	RCL	10	04	4
03	04	4	07	02	2	11	41	R/S

*Denotes 2nd function key

LOC	CODE	KEY	LOC	CODE	KEY	LOC	CODE	KEY
12	34	RCL	37	64	×	62	94	=
13	03	3	38	01	1	63	59	*pause
14	57	*subr	39	00	0	64	59	*pause
15	04	4	40	00	0	65	28	* | x |
16	04	4	41	94	=	66	35	SUM
17	41	R/S	42	41	R/S	67	00	0
18	34	RCL	43	42	RST	68	58	*rtn
19	04	4	44	57	*subr	69	33	STO
20	57	*subr	45	06	6	70	07	7
21	04	4	46	09	9	71	29	*Int
22	04	4	47	39	*EXC	72	64	×
23	41	R/S	48	08	8	73	06	6
24	34	RCL	49	57	*subr	74	00	0
25	05	5	50	06	6	75	94	=
26	57	*subr	51	09	9	76	84	+
27	04	4	52	35	SUM	77	34	RCL
28	04	4	53	08	8	78	07	7
29	41	R/S	54	34	RCL	79	12	INV
30	34	RCL	55	09	9	80	29	*Int
31	06	6	56	57	*subr	81	64	×
32	57	*subr	57	06	6	82	01	1
33	04	4	58	09	9	83	00	0
34	04	4	59	74	−	84	00	0
35	34	RCL	60	34	RCL	85	94	=
36	00	0	61	08	8	86	58	*rtn

SR-56 Scoring Program II

Program Note

If there are fewer than six rally legs to be scored, the program must be modified. To avoid confusion, we suggest that you store the program exactly as it is printed and then adjust it in this way:

Number of legs to be scored	In execute mode, press:
5	GTO 29 LRN GTO 35 LRN RST
4	GTO 23 LRN GTO 35 LRN RST
3	GTO 17 LRN GTO 35 LRN RST
2	GTO 11 LRN GTO 35 LRN RST

---

*Denotes 2nd function key

Data Entries

Key in the allowed leg times as hours, decimal point, minutes and hundredths:

Leg 1	STO 1	Leg 4	STO 4
Leg 2	STO 2	Leg 5	STO 5
Leg 3	STO 3	Leg 6	STO 6

Program Execution

Key in Car 1's leg 1 starting time as hours, decimal point, minutes and hundredths and press STO 8; key in Car 1's leg 1 finishing time in the same units and press STO 9; press RST R/S.

The pause at steps 63-64 displays the *time error* in minutes and hundredths (with a minus sign if the car was early).

When the program has run, key in Car 1's leg 2 starting time STO 8 and its leg 2 finishing time STO 9 R/S (do *not* press RST!).

Repeat the procedure until Car 1's last leg has been scored. The display is then Car 1's total penalty.

Press 0 STO 0; R_0 now *must* be cleared.

Proceed to score Car 2 in the same fashion.

SR-56 SCORING PROGRAM IIA

Scores one car at a time for up to six legs at one point per hundredth of a minute early or late, with a maximum penalty for lateness

LOC	CODE	KEY	LOC	CODE	KEY	LOC	CODE	KEY
00	57	*subr	11	09	9	22	93	+/−
01	05	5	12	57	*subr	23	24	×
02	00	0	13	05	5	24	01	1
03	39	*EXC	14	00	0	25	00	0
04	08	8	15	74	−	26	00	0
05	57	*subr	16	34	RCL	27	94	=
06	05	5	17	08	8	28	59	*pause
07	00	0	18	94	=	29	59	*pause
08	35	SUM	19	47	*$x \geq t$	30	35	SUM
09	08	8	20	03	3	31	00	0
10	34	RCL	21	07	7	32	34	RCL

*Denotes 2nd function key

LOC	CODE	KEY	LOC	CODE	KEY	LOC	CODE	KEY
33	00	0	45	03	3	57	84	+
34	56	*CP	46	32	$x \leq t$	58	34	RCL
35	41	R/S	47	22	GTO	59	07	7
36	42	RST	48	02	2	60	12	INV
37	32	$x \leq t$	49	03	3	61	29	*Int
38	00	0	50	33	STO	62	64	×
39	05	5	51	07	7	63	01	1
40	47	*$x \geq t$	52	29	*Int	64	00	0
41	04	4	53	64	×	65	00	0
42	06	6	54	06	6	66	94	=
43	22	GTO	55	00	0	67	58	*rtn
44	02	2	56	94	=			

SR-56 Scoring Program IIA

Program Notes

Locations 38-39 store in program memory the maximum late time in whole minutes. As the program is printed here, the max is 05 minutes. It can of course be any number of minutes from 01 − 99. If there is no maximum, do not attempt to store 00; 99 would be a better choice. But it would be best to make use of Program II, which, since it includes no tests for maximum lateness, has steps available for advancing the calculator automatically to the next leg to be scored.

If there are fewer than six legs to score, nothing in the program needs to be changed. The display at the end of each program run always gives the car's cumulative point score.

Data Entries

Key in the allowed times as hours, decimal point, minutes and hundredths:

Leg 1	STO 1		Leg 4	STO 4
Leg 2	STO 2		Leg 5	STO 5
Leg 3	STO 3		Leg 6	STO 6

---

*Denotes 2nd function key

Program Execution

Key in Car 1's leg 1 starting time as hours, decimal point, minutes, hundredths and press STO 8; key in Car 1's leg 1 finishing time in the same units and press STO 9.

Now press *fix 0 RST RCL 1 R/S. The first display, at steps 28 − 29, shows the *time error* in minutes and hundredths (with a minus sign if the car was early). The display at step 35 shows the accumulated point penalty.

Key in Car 1's leg 2 starting time STO 8, and the finishing time STO 9.

Press RCL 2 R/S. The first display shows the leg 2 time error, and the display at step 35 shows the accumulated point penalty.

Score the remaining legs in the same way. When the last leg has been scored and the total penalty points have been recorded, press 0 STO 0. The calculator is now ready to score Car 2.

SR-56 CHECK POINT BY CHECK POINT SCORING PROGRAM III

Scores one leg at a time at one point per hundredth of a minute early or late with a flat maximum penalty of 5 minutes or 500 points

LOC	CODE	KEY	LOC	CODE	KEY	LOC	CODE	KEY
						35	05	5
00	93	+/−	18	94	=	36	33	STO
01	57	*subr	19	59	*pause	37	09	9
03	06	6	20	59	*pause	38	29	*Int
04	39	*EXC	21	28	$*\lvert x \rvert$	39	64	×
05	00	0	22	47	$*x \geq t$	40	06	6
06	57	*subr	23	03	3	41	00	0
07	03	3	24	02	2	42	94	=
08	06	6	25	64	×	43	84	+
09	35	SUM	26	01	1	44	34	RCL
10	00	0	27	00	0	45	09	9
11	05	5	28	00	0	46	12	INV
12	32	$x \leq t$	29	94	=	47	29	*Int
13	34	RCL	30	41	R/S	48	64	×
14	00	0	31	42	RST	49	01	1
15	84	+	32	32	$x \leq t$	50	00	0
16	34	RCL	33	22	GTO	51	00	0
17	01	1	34	02	2	52	94	=
						53	58	*rtn

*Denotes 2nd function key

SR-56 Scoring Program II

Data Entry

Key in the allowed time for the leg to be scored as *minutes, decimal point, hundredths of minutes* and press STO 1.

Program Execution

1. RST
2. Key in Car 1's starting time as *hours, decimal point, hundredths of minutes* and press STO 0.
3. Key in Car 1's finishing time in the same units and press R/S.
4. The pause at steps 19 − 20 displays the time error in minutes and hundredths (negative if the car was late).
5. The second, final display shows the penalty points at 1 point per hundredth of a minute (maximum penalty 500 points).
6. To score Car 2 for the same leg, key in the starting time, press STO 0, key in the finishing time, press R/S.
7. To score Car 1 for Leg 2, store the allowed time in R_1 and repeat program execution steps 2 − 6.

Postscript

IF YOU ARE wondering whether the rally navigation and scoring programs outlined here are the only ones that can be written for the HP-25 and the SR-56, the answer is no. The simplest of arithmetical problems can be written down and solved in several ways. When it comes to synthesizing more complex operations for processing by calculator, there are, in spite of certain strictures, a great many options.

If these are not the only programs, are they then the best ones possible? We'd of course like to think so, but that is really a nonquestion with no answer, because to define a "best" program is virtually impossible. Any calculator or computer program that produces the right answer is a good one. Another program, if it gives the right answer in fewer steps and therefore more quickly, or if it is easier to use, deserves to be called "better." But as long as there is any possibility of making a good program better, and a better one even better than that, there can be no "best." The rally programs in this book do give the right answers; however, if you prefer to take your own, different approach, there is nothing to prevent you from amending them, modifying them or altogether rewriting them to your particular purposes.

And what about other calculators, since the HP-25 and the SR-56 are not the only pocket programmables on the market? It is unlikely that other makes and models will be able to use these programs exactly as written, but it should not be difficult to adapt the HP-25 programs to any RPN calculator and the SR-56 programs to any AN calculator.

Finally, although this book has treated the two calculators—and the two kinds of calculators—fairly comprehensively, it could not, obviously, deal with these particular applications and at the same time duplicate the wealth of information contained in the 112-page HP-25 Owner's Handbook, the 161-page HP-25 Applications Programs book, the 122-page SR-56 Owner's Manual and the 192-page SR-56 Applications Library. We urge you to study the books that are part of your calculator kit. They won't tell you a thing about rallying, but they will tell you ever so many things about your calculator that will enhance its value to you in rallying—and in countless other ways.

Index

A
Algebraic notation SR-56   101
Arithmetic
  navigational HP-25   32
  navigational SR-56   120
  storage-register HP-25   24
Automatic memory stack HP-25   22
Average-speed navigation
  HP-25 program I   57
  HP-25 program II   61
  HP-25 program III   63
  SR-56   143

B
Branching
  conditional HP-25   48
  unconditional HP-25   46

C
Calculating, HP-25   30
Calculations, SR-56   118
Clear, HP-25   85
Conditional branching, HP-25   48
Constructing program, SR-56   128
Correction factors
  HP-25   34
  SR-56   122

D
Data entries, HP-25   45, 51
Display
  HP-25   28
  SR-56   115
Distance units, HP-25   65

E
Equations
  analyzing, HP-25   37
  time-speed-distance, HP-25   32
  tine-speed-distance, SR-56   120

F
Formulas, analyzing, HP-25   37

H
Harmonic mean
  HP-25   36
  SR-56   123
Hewlett-Packard HP-25 programmable pocket calculator   15
HP-25   15
  automatic memory stack   22
  average-speed navigation program I   57
  average-speed navigation program II   61
  average-speed navigation program III   63
  calculating   30
  checkpoint-by-checkpoint scoring   98
  clear   85
  display   28
  keyboard   16
  keycodes   16
  maximum-penalty scoring program IA   91
  percentages   38
  power supply   28
  programming   42
  rally navigation   54
  rally programs, testing   73
  registers   22
  scoring program I   88
  switches   21

I
Iterative programs, HP-25   46

K
Keyboard, SR-56   104
Keycodes
  HP-25   16
  SR-56 program   105

L
Last-X register, HP-25   25

M

Memory
- registers, SR-56   116
- storage registers, HP-25   23

N

Navigation, HP-25 rally   54
Navigational arithmetic
- HP-25   32
- SR-56   120

Negative values, HP-25   45

O

Odometer check
- HP-25   34, 63
- SR-56   121

Odometer, SR-56   121

P

Percentages, HP-25   38
Perfecting a program, SR-56   130
Phantom car problems
- HP-25   38
- SR-56   125

Power supply, HP-25   21, 28
Problems, special SR-56   123
Program
- building, HP-25   42
- checking, HP-25   44
- constructing, SR-56   128
- debugging, HP-25   44
- initialization, HP-25   45
- iterative, HP-25   46
- perfecting, SR-56   130
- step register, HP-25   24
- registers, SR-56   116

Programmability, SR-56   101
Programming
- HP-25   42
- SR-56   127

R

Rally
- navigation programs, SR-56   139
- programs, SR-56, testing   163
- scoring programs for the HP-25   87

Registers
- HP-25   22
- last-x HP-25   25
- memory storage, HP-25   23
- program SR-56   116
- program-step, HP-25   24
- SR-56   115, 116
- T SR-56   117

Reverse Polish notation, HP-25   25
Routines, time-conversion SR-56   134

S

Scoring
- HP-25 checkpoint-by-checkpoint   98
- HP-25 maximum-penalty   91
- HP-25 program I   88

Scoring program
- checking out SR-56   187
- SR-56   183

Simulatneous displays   161
- HP-25   69

Speed
- changing, HP-25   84
- changing, SR-56   177

SR-56
- average-speed navigation   143
- calculating   118
- checking out scoring programs   187
- clear   181
- constructing programs   128
- display   115
- keyboard   104
- program keycode   105
- programming   127
- programmability   101
- rally navigation programs   139
- rally programs, testing   163
- registers   115
- scoring program   183
- simultaneous displays   161
- speed changing   177
- supplementary routine   157
- switches   113
- time-based route directions   156

Storage-register, arithmetic, HP-25   24
Subroutines, SR-56   137
Supplementary routine, SR-56   157
Switches
- HP-25   21
- SR-56   113

T

Texas Instruments SR-56 programmable pocket calculator   101
Time-based route directions, HP-25   66
Time-conversion routines, SR-56   134
Time-speed-distance, SR-56   120
T-registers, SR-56   117

U

Unconditional branching, HP-25   46

About the Author

LARRY REID and his wife, Joan, commenced rallying in 1952 and competed regularly for more than fifteen years, meeting with a fair share of successes, as evidenced by several shelffuls of trophies that Joan still polishes regularly.

Larry co-founded the Touring Club of New England, a Boston-based rally club, in 1953. He served for four years as its secretary-treasurer and editor of its newsletter, *Driver & Navigator*, and he wrote the TCNE rally handbook. Later he was elected TCNE's president for a year's term. He is the club's honorary life secretary.

As a member of the Sports Car Club of America, he served in the mid-nineteen-fifties as New England Region rally chairman, secretary and regional executive (president). In 1963 he headed the committee that drew up the Region's rally rules and regulations. He also officiated at many SCCA regional and national sports car races as flagman, timer and scorer, and race chairman. He was appointed to the SCCA Rally Board on its creation in 1957 and was its chairman in 1961 and 1962. He was four times chairman of the Berkshire National Rally. He was named to the SCCA Planning Committee in 1963 and was reappointed in 1964.

Since giving up active competition and club work, the Reids have made nine tours, with car and camera, of Great Britain and western Europe. Long-time residents of Boston, they retired in mid-1977 and moved to a house they had built near St. Augustine, Florida.

Larry is the author of four other books on rallying, all well known. Of this, his latest, he says: "Not so many years ago I proclaimed publicly and confidently that an electronic calculator suitable for rally navigation would have to be carried about in a ten-ton truck. So much for *that* crystal ball!"